D0615528

FEB 2 8 2020

At the
CENTER
of All
BEAUTY

ALSO BY FENTON JOHNSON

Crossing the River

Scissors, Paper, Rock

Geography of the Heart: A Memoir

*Keeping Faith: A Skeptic's Journey among
Christian and Buddhist Monks*

The Man Who Loved Birds

Everywhere Home: A Life in Essays

At the
CENTER
of All
BEAUTY

*Solitude and
the Creative Life*

FENTON JOHNSON

W. W. NORTON & COMPANY
Independent Publishers Since 1923

Copyright © 2020 by Fenton Johnson

All rights reserved
Printed in the United States of America
First Edition

For information about permission to reproduce selections from this book,
write to Permissions, W. W. Norton & Company, Inc.,
500 Fifth Avenue, New York, NY 10110

For information about special discounts for bulk purchases, please contact
W. W. Norton Special Sales at specialsales@wwnorton.com or 800-233-4830

Manufacturing by LSC Communications, Harrisonburg
Book design by Ellen Cipriano
Production manager: Lauren Abbate

Library of Congress Cataloging-in-Publication Data

Names: Johnson, Fenton, author.
Title: At the center of all beauty : solitude and
the creative life / Fenton Johnson.
Description: First edition. | New York : W. W. Norton & Company, [2020]
Identifiers: LCCN 2019044449 | ISBN 9780393608298 (hardcover) |
ISBN 9780393608304 (epub)
Subjects: LCSH: Solitude. | Personality and creative ability. |
Creation (Literary, artistic, etc.) | Johnson, Fenton. |
Gay men—United States—Biography.
Classification: LCC BF637.S64 J64 2020 | DDC 155.9/2—dc23
LC record available at https://lccn.loc.gov/2019044449

W. W. Norton & Company, Inc., 500 Fifth Avenue, New York, N.Y. 10110
www.wwnorton.com

W. W. Norton & Company Ltd., 15 Carlisle Street, London W1D 3BS

1 2 3 4 5 6 7 8 9 0

For Paul Quenon
poet, rascal, friend, monk

And here I am, the
center of all beauty!
writing these poems!
Imagine!

—Frank O'Hara, "Autobiographia Literaria"

I was always my own teacher.

—Eudora Welty, *One Writer's Beginnings*

CONTENTS

CHAPTER 1

Monks and Rascals   1

CHAPTER 2

The Forging of a Solitary   16

CHAPTER 3

I to Myself *(Henry David Thoreau)*   39

CHAPTER 4

The Psychology of the Earth *(Paul Cézanne)*   53

CHAPTER 5

Formidably Alone *(Walt Whitman and Emily Dickinson)* 73

CHAPTER 6

The Generosity of Bachelors *(Henry James)*   95

CHAPTER 7

All Serious Daring Begins Within *(Eudora Welty)*   107

CHAPTER 8

The Lover of God *(Rabindranath Tagore)*   128

CHAPTER 9

A Soundless Island in a Tideless Sea *(Zora Neale Hurston)*   157

CHAPTER 10

A Man Alone, A Single Woman *(Rod McKuen
and Nina Simone)*   168

CHAPTER 11

Those Who Seek Beauty Will Find It *(Bill Cunningham)*   185

CHAPTER 12

From Loneliness to Solitude   201

ACKNOWLEDGMENTS AND THANKS   235

PERMISSIONS   237

At the
CENTER
of All
BEAUTY

CHAPTER 1

Monks and Rascals

IN MY SEVENTH GRADE, on a spring day deep in the Kentucky hills, aged and tremulous Sister Marie-Thérèse (with the dead-on cruelty of children, we nicknamed her "B.C.") assigned us to draw posters illustrating some important principle from our Roman Catholic catechism. I chose to draw "Three Roads to Heaven," illustrating a page from the chapter on vocations—life callings; the word owes itself to the Latin verb *vocare*, "to call."

A series of coincidences—if such exist—has brought that poster across forty-plus years of time and a thousand miles of space to hang on my office wall. In it I drew the path of life leading through a field of smudges toward a heaven of puffy clouds—the smudges had been yellow tulips, but Sister Marie-Thérèse, an intelligent woman born to a hardscrabble rural life and thus one who would know, declared there were *no yellow tulips on the road to heaven* and hovered, rubber-tipped pointer poised to strike at any sign of resistance, while I erased them one by one.

Where the field ended, I drew two footprints pausing before a question mark. The road forks into three paths, each leading to one of the three church-designated callings. The leftmost path leads to THE RELIGIOUS LIFE, where I drew a cloud enclosing a cross, a priest's biretta, and a book labeled *Divine Office*. The middle path leads to MARRIAGE, whose cloud encloses a wedding ring, a baby bassinet labeled *Junior*, and a page from a legal contract (how prescient I was!). The rightmost path leads to a cloud labeled SINGLE, which our catechism offered as a legitimate calling, officially on a par with the other two options. I recall an evening spent trying to conceive a visual metaphor for the solitary life. Finally I settled on a series of musical notes dancing over the caption *Party Time!*

Well into midlife, what I find most remarkable about that poster is my catechism's teaching that being single was a legitimate vocation, i.e., like the religious life, like marriage, a response to a particular and urgent summons from a force greater than individual need or choice—a summons, as you wish, from destiny, from the gods and goddesses, from God. That the growing good of the universe includes—indeed, requires—solitaries is a revolutionary teaching. The Hebrew Bible hasn't much to say on the subject, but the cultural imperative in Judaism to marry and bear children is as strong, possibly stronger even than in Hinduism. Islam views solitaries as shirkers at best, troublemakers at worst. Buddhism grounds itself in monastic practice—solitaries living in community—but presumes that anyone living outside that community will marry.

Another remarkable aspect of that poster: at twelve years old, I already knew which path had chosen me. Father Gettelfinger, even more aged than Sister Marie-Thérèse, asked each student in my class. I was the only one to respond, "Single."

Popular culture tells us that, even in our postmodern age, being single is "party time" (see my poster) for people in their teens and twenties. After that, "single" is a way-station until marriage, or between marriages, or a dumping-ground designation for those unable to attract a mate, or those who are "too picky," or those who are so sexually repressed or ravenous or selfish that they can't submit to the civilizing bonds of conventional marriage, which (*pace* Freud) is the most healthy option and the most selfless path an individual may follow.

Or such was the myth, until now. We are in the midst of a demographic revolution whose long-term implications may be as significant as the twentieth century's mass migration from the countryside to the city. I speak of the astonishing numbers of people worldwide who are choosing to live alone or who deliberately carve out periods of solitude from otherwise conventionally coupled lives. The evidence is accumulating that when people, especially women, are presented with the opportunity and the means to live alone, many will sacrifice to seize it.

That the number of solitaries is growing worldwide is without question, but we have made little acknowledgment and accommodation of that fact. Our housing, health care, and urban planning—everything from restaurant design to discount gym memberships to the gargantuan loaves of bread our bakeries turn out—is still based on the ideal of the coupled household, preferably with two children. Of greatest consequence, the stories we tell ourselves embody fantasies of idealized couples and families, even if in unconventional configurations, instead of the rich and rewarding solitary journeys more and more of us are living out.

Some see in this development a sign of social breakdown. I look at this demographic transformation and see not the crumbling of the cornerstone of society, but the potential for more diverse and loving relationships to one another and to our planet. With 7.5 billion-plus people on the earth, surely solitaries—especially those who are childless or who adopt—offer alternative stories worth our attention and support. In my case, early in my twenties I realized that, with many nieces and nephews already born and more likely to arrive, the planet had no shortage of my particular genetic material. In a world groaning under the weight of too many people, I would undertake the second most selfless act I could imagine: I would remain child-less. I would do my best to serve others as a teacher and writer.

Perhaps some deep wisdom is manifesting itself in these mil-lions of people seeking, or at least experiencing, solitude. Perhaps solitaries are evidence of an aspect of the human character only now permitted to blossom. If one subscribes to the Western conception of progress—that it is possible to study our past, learn from it, and apply those lessons to build a better future—maybe studying the works and lives of our solitaries is key to reconceiving our understanding of the human family.

And so I find myself well along in life and living alone, a state of affairs I have come to embrace as the way things ought to be. I have dated many men and a few women in my life, and count myself lucky to have met and come to know almost every one of them. I have had many enduring friendships and at least one, arguably two great loves, and though one of those loves had the misfortune to die young, that does not for a moment undercut our great good fortune in having found each other, a stroke of luck he marveled at almost daily, in the course of teaching me a lesson about the present-tense nature of love that I learned in the hardest possible way—a love that gave me and the world a book. The men and women of my intimate past with whom I've stayed in touch—I try to stay present to my past—have in most cases found partners who are, I joke, so clearly better suited to them that they reinforce my sense that I was meant to be alone— meant to be a monadnock, a solitary mountain.

One could argue, of course, that marriages are not found but made, and that had I stuck by someone or someone had stuck by me, we might have one of those relationships that, at least from the outside, appears ordained. I think not. Like getting married or professing a vocation to religion, living alone results from complicated, interlocking factors and decisions, made or avoided. Some of us were born to be solitaries—some were from birth "not the marrying kind," as my grandmother so presciently said of me, a line both Bette Davis in *Now, Voyager* and Cary Grant in *Indiscreet* use to describe themselves. Many of us have arrived at our solitude as a result of circumstance—as who does not arrive at any place in life as a result of circumstance? Some gave our hearts away, to find that once given away they were not so easily recovered. Some are widowed. Some are shy—physically or emotionally daunted by the nakedness, literal and emotional, of intimate contact. Many women live alone because the taboos against divorce and raising children alone have relaxed. Life has not presented them with a suitable mate and they are sufficiently financially secure, or willing to endure financial insecurity, to live alone or, if they choose, to adopt and/or give birth without a mate. Gay men and lesbians who once married as a necessary cover can now live alone and have fulfilling relationships with friends and lovers. Some men and women prefer to devote themselves to public service or to lives in the arts or education. Some decide to replenish the wellspring of a relationship through spending time alone. Some live out more than one of these ways of being, at different points in their lives. And then there are those who share the defiant spirit of Prometheus, he who stole fire from the gods and declared he would rather be chained to a rock and tortured daily than submit to their will. He was among our first solitaries.

All these are, to my imagination, rich, important, true ways to live, even as they represent radical departures from conventional norms into largely unexplored social and emotional territories, amid a rising cacophony of social media that ten years ago didn't exist, an avalanche of technology hell-bent on ensuring that we are never, ever alone.

I am writing, not about what pop culture and demographers call "singles"—a word that means nothing outside the context of marriage—but about *solitaries*, to use the term favored by the Trappist monk and mystic Thomas Merton. Merton's use of the word "solitary," unlike "bachelor" or "spinster" or "single," is independent of connotations of gender and sex and doesn't carry the opprobrium of centuries of marriage-focused mythologies. A friend, a lifelong solitary, objected. "That word sounds so—*solitary*," she said. "Exactly so," I responded. "Solitary" evokes not the trees of the forest, beautiful as they may be, but the twisted pine that through persistence and strength of character has found purchase on a rocky crag; or a great blue heron standing in a pool of crystalline water, the very definition of here and now, the patient present moment; or Paul Cézanne's Mont Sainte-Victoire, the holy mountain of triumph, rising in solitary splendor above the plain of Provence. Indeed, like the heron or the mountain, we are loners, though I do not use the word, much as I like it, because of the negative connotations it has been assigned; descriptions of mass murderers almost always include it, even when the murderer turns out to be married.

To define a solitary as someone who is not married—to define solitude as the absence of coupling—is like defining silence as the absence of noise. Solitude and silence are positive gestures. This is why Buddhists say we can learn what we need to know sitting on the cushion. This is why I say you can learn what you need to know from the silent, solitary disciplines of reading and writing, the consciously chosen, deliberately inhabited discipline of silence.

What, then, defines a solitary? Solitaries have no piece of paper in the city hall, to quote Joni Mitchell, herself no stranger to solitude; we have no church or government certification and sanction of our status. We certify it in our hearts and for ourselves; we live it out. We are different from the rest—something odd about us, apt to go off and meditate and muse in solitude.

I write for you, my fellow traveler, my intimate for the next few minutes or hours; for you, my solitary friend. I recognize you when we encounter each other: alone on the hiking trail, alone in a museum, alone in a church, alone in your choice of the solitude of reading over the cacophony of voices and images available through online chat and distraction; alone in your room.

But now we come to a koan—in Zen Buddhism, a question or quandary to be contemplated in solitude and silence. What figure does the solitary cut in the human tapestry? What is the usefulness of sitting alone writing, or painting, or reading, or watching the changing light? What is the usefulness of the *flâneur*, the solitary walker in the city streets or the autumn forest? What is the usefulness of the solitary—most especially the childless solitary—whose very existence points to the biggest question: Absent reproduction—which, after all, bacteria accomplish more efficiently than human beings—what is the usefulness of life?

Go to any bookstore and you'll find shelves of books written about living in relationship—how to find a relationship, how to hold one together once it's found, how to survive its falling apart, how to find one again. Churches offer classes, preachers preach, therapists counsel about how to get and stay coupled. Then go looking for books about how to live alone. You will be searching for a long while, even though worldwide more and more of us are living alone.

And yet your bookstore search will reveal that, of the classic works of literature on the shelves, a remarkable number will have been written by people who lived alone for most of their lives or who had no semblance of a conventional coupled relationship. Evidently some visceral impulse impels us solitaries to sing—to offer our gifts to others seeking—or at least, in the course of their reading, experiencing—solitude.

In search of a rich, life-affirming perspective on my solitary life, I began to actively seek out the works, lives, homes, and studios of solitary writers and artists, with the hope of learning and passing on what they teach about the dignity and rewards of being alone. As I spent more and more time with these writers and artists, I found them speaking to me—haunting me—appearing as visions and voices, urging me onward, telling me that I was *getting them right,* in understanding their solitude not as tragedy or bad luck or loneliness but as an integral and necessary aspect of who they were. In their work and stories they spoke as witnesses in a great cloud around me: Henry David Thoreau ("the man who goes alone can start today; but he who travels with another must wait til that other is ready, and it may be a long time before they get off"), Louisa May Alcott ("I prefer to be a free spinster and paddle my own canoe"), Amelia Earhart, in her wedding letter to her husband ("I may have to keep some place where I can go to be by myself now and then, for I cannot guarantee to endure at all the confinements of even an attractive cage").

To write about solitaries and solitude is to be required to invent or repurpose language. We have few words to describe and express solitude, restraint, obliquity. Asked to describe her loves, the solitary must use the language of blood kin, of marriage, of family. We have few words unique to friendship. In describing that all-important relationship, we must use language intended to describe relationships sanctioned and governed by church and state, or the language of sexual passion. To speak of celibacy, we describe it not in terms of what it is, but of what it is not—not sex, not fun, not hip, not done.

Throughout this book I liberate the words "bachelor" and "spinster" from their pejorative connotations and restore to them the dignity of their roots in honest labor: *bachelor,* from Old French *bacheler,* a knight or squire in service to a greater cause; *spinster,* an unmarried woman who made her living by spinning fiber into thread, bringing warmth and pleasure to our naked lives. Unless otherwise indicated, with occasional exceptions for snippets of analysis, almost all the writers, composers, and artists profiled or quoted in these pages are, by my definition, solitaries—individuals who, through a combination of temperament, chance, and choice, of discipline, fate, and free will, chose solitude as their means of giving themselves to others.

Here is a great secret, seldom acknowledged in popular culture: it is possible to be a solitary within a couple. In fact, the most successful couples of my acquaintance are composed of solitaries leading parallel lives, who understand both the rewards and responsibilities of being together and the rewards and responsibilities of being apart. In a letter to his friend Margaret Staats, Nobel-winning novelist Saul Bellow, married five times, wrote, "One of my friends tells me, truly, that I am the solitary of solitaries, a combination of a glacier and a volcano, that I have perfected the power to be alone." Later in the same letter, he added, "It seems that I never have accepted my condition. The making of an artist: seven decades of work without being reconciled to the essential facts of my condition."

"The making of an artist": it is the struggle with and in solitude that defines the artist, regardless of whether she publishes books or arranges flowers or shows paintings or performs music. To be an artist is not, finally, about product; it is about process, a way of being, and every solitary is of necessity an artist—an artist of her or his life, with little or no help from conventional rites and forms and mythologies, making it up as we go.

The women and men whom I have read and studied were not hermits, much as I respect hermitry as a path. Paul Cézanne was not, to use the language of our current, narrow understanding of human relationship, "single"—he had a long-lasting if stormy relationship with Marie-Hortense Fiquet, who bore his son and whom he eventually married—but he was a solitary, someone who found his greatest satisfaction and fulfillment in solitude. Few people have maintained social calendars as full as that of Henry James. Zora Neale Hurston married three times, though she never cohabited for more than a few months and spent more time extricating herself from her marriages than living within them. Thoreau, so often cited as the high priest of solitude, entertained a stream of visitors at his Walden Pond cabin, and on days when no one visited he walked into town. Some of my solitaries lived with relatives—the writers Emily Dickinson and Eudora Welty, Thoreau in the last decade of his short life, the artists Giorgio Morandi and Joseph Cornell. Some had brief, intermittent affairs, even as they lived primarily in and for solitude—the poet Walt Whitman comes to mind. Though Thomas Merton may be our most eloquent modern writer on solitude, he lived in a community of monks with whom he regularly worshipped and communicated, he maintained a voluminous correspondence with writers and thinkers worldwide, he extended visits to nearby Louisville for medical appointments so as to visit with friends, he entertained visitors at his hermitage.

In the following pages I converse with these writers and artists through their work—the surest and most profound way that they remain alive to us. Joseph Conrad wrote that "the writer of imaginative prose stands confessed in his works"; Henry James, his friend, that the writer is present in "every page of every book from which he sought so assiduously to eliminate himself." In their work, my solitaries reveal their most intimate selves.

I have turned to writers and artists as seemingly different as Henry David Thoreau and Nina Simone, Henry James and Zora Neale Hurston, not because they are exceptionally perceptive—I have met perceptive people in every profession, from plumbing to the law—but because we leave records of our lives, and because being a writer or an artist demands that we develop a relationship with our solitude. Growing older and deeper into my own solitude, I began to see my solitaries as role models for the cultivation of an interior life; as role models for leading the fruitful, engaged life of a solitary. Far from being the parched and desiccate creatures of myth and gossip, my solitaries are so alive to the world—so sensitive to its nuance and turnings—that they're incapable of limiting themselves to one person or one household. My solitaries are votaries, living at the center of beauty.

My mother carried a walking stick on every hike, even in the days when her balance was fine and before her knees gave out. "To turn over things to see what lies underneath," she said, and demonstrated by turning over a rock. Underneath was a bright-ribboned, iridescent skink.

From her I learned to turn over other, less tangible things—assumptions we make about who we are and how we relate to one another. A country woman who lived alone for the last twenty-five years of her life, she taught by example about solitude and the importance and beauty of silence, in a society dedicated to making noise.

"There is a long history of gay isolation," writes a solitary scholar friend. Of course he is correct. One might say that solitude is, though not unique to LGBT people, at least a homeland—maybe our true homeland. But consider the testimony of Elizabeth Cady Stanton, pioneering women's rights activist, contentedly married, mother of seven, before the U.S. Senate Committee on Women's Suffrage in 1898:

> Think for a moment of the immeasurable solitude of self. We come into the world alone, unlike all who have gone before us, we leave it alone, under circumstances peculiar to ourselves. . . .
>
> . . . When death sunders our nearest ties, alone we sit in the shadow of our affliction. Alike amid the greatest triumphs and darkest tragedies of life, we walk alone. On the divine heights of human attainment, eulogized and worshipped as a hero or saint, we stand alone. In ignorance, poverty and vice, as a pauper or criminal, alone we starve or steal; alone we suffer the sneers and rebuffs of our fellows; alone we are hunted and hounded through dark courts and alleys, in by-ways and high-ways; alone we stand in the judgment seat; alone in the prison cell we lament our crimes and misfortunes; alone we expiate them on the gallows. In hours like these we realize the awful solitude of individual life, its pains, its penalties, its responsibilities . . .
>
> . . . there is a solitude which each and every one of us has always carried with him, more inaccessible than the ice-cold mountains, more profound than the midnight sea: the solitude of self. . . . to it only omniscience is permitted to enter.
>
> Such is individual life.

Frequently I overhear or read pundits or scholars who perceive unhappiness as inherent in the disintegration of traditional families and small-town community life, and indeed there is a *loneliness* that arises from our capitalist, consumerist, addictive, wired society. That loneliness arises, I suggest, because we are looking outside to assuage a longing that can only be addressed within—through turning over the stone of our loneliness, to perceive it instead as solitude.

Surely those who have the most profound experience of solitude may have the most to teach. I mean not only the writers and artists profiled in these pages, or LGBT people, but also the recently divorced woman, the postpartum mother, the grieving spouse, the terminally ill, the homeless—all those who suffer and who, for the duration of their suffering, whether it be a month or a year or a lifetime, are outliers, outsiders, outcasts.

A *Wounded* deer leaps highest . . .

Emily Dickinson [#165]

In his impressions of the earliest decades of the American Empire and its grand experiment with democracy, the Frenchman Alexis de Tocqueville wrote, "Thus . . . democracy . . . continually turns man back into himself and threatens at last to enclose him entirely in the solitude of his own heart." Tocqueville implies that this outcome is pernicious, isolating us one from another. But, ever my mother's son, I turn over the rock of isolation, to find underneath the challenge and solace of solitude.

Is it significant that Tocqueville, a man, perceives solitude as democracy's dark side, where Elizabeth Cady Stanton perceives it as democracy's precondition? Might their difference root itself in part in their gender? Stanton is not advocating hermitry. Instead she is arguing that, given that the development of inner resources is essential to individual well-being, society must offer people of all genders equal treatment before its law, from which foundation each individual may undertake her or his necessarily individual, solitary journey.

> No persons are free who will not dare to pursue the questions
> of their own loneliness. It is through them that they live.
>
> Christopher Fry

If the journey through our interior landscape is so critical to our characters, let us become more informed and responsible travelers. Let us start by turning off our phones and spending more time alone. Let us start by studying solitaries and solitude.

CHAPTER 2

The Forging of a Solitary

MINE WAS NOT, I came to understand much later, a commonplace childhood, but was instead a crucible for the forging of a solitary. Trappist monks from the nearby Abbey of Gethsemani and my parents were my first role models. Ours was a medieval landscape, a chunk of Normandy transplanted by the improbable forces of history to the Kentucky Knobs. As recently as my childhood, the Gethsemani Trappists spoke in hand gestures and farmed with great draft horses, waking or leaving off their work to pray the offices when the tower bell tolled: Vigils at 3 a.m., then Lauds, Tierce, Sext, None, Vespers at sunset, Compline to close the day, the church dark except for a candlelit icon, *o clement, o precious, o sweet Virgin Mary, give us a restful night and a peaceful death.* Chaucer would have been puzzled by the noisy, farting internal combustion engine––the abbey sold its draft horses and introduced tractors in the 1950s—but otherwise he could have found among the people of my rural Kentucky countryside his Manciple, his Merchant, his Squire, his Man of Law, his Plowman, his Reeve, his Wife of Bath, and me, his Clerk.

True to its Norman roots, the abbey kept a dairy herd and,

throughout my childhood, made and sold cheese, a product that met the mail-order requirement that it improve, not deteriorate, with age. Brother Fintan, an amiable Irish-American alcoholic looking for a way to spirit spirits into the enclosure, undertook to add a second mail-order product that improved with age: his grandmother's bourbon-soaked fruitcake. My father, who oversaw maintenance at a small Seagram distillery, became the conduit for bourbon from the distillery to the monastery, along the way making himself popular with the monks by misplacing a few bottles.

Cloistered monasteries, however isolated from mainstream culture, are in fact its microcosm—the great forces that manifest themselves in the streets and fields, and on the evening news, shape and direct life inside the walls as well. The 1960s and 1970s were a time of iconoclasm inside as well as outside the monastery, with the abbots of those tumultuous years more relaxed than their predecessors or successors in allowing interaction between the monks and nearby communities. The "choir monks"—the educated monks, among them Thomas Merton, known to us as Father Louis—ventured to Louisville and beyond to let down their tonsured hair; when they needed a respite from contemplative life, they sought out civilization and its comforts. But the "lay monks"—the field laborers—moved discreetly but more or less freely among the villagers. Thus began a decade—coincident with the years of my growing up—in which Trappist monks regularly found their way over the hills to my parents' house, always arriving just before supper.

It is a source of lifelong bemusement that I am named for the two monks who made the Abbey of Gethsemani one of the world's most financially stable monasteries. Eight children into their marriage and at a loss for names, my parents handed me over to the monks for naming. A man way ahead of his time, Brother Clement, whose birth name was John, introduced mail-order purchase of cheese; then Brother Fintan added his grandmother's fruitcake to the catalogue. And so I became John Fenton, after my mother drew the line at "Clement"—"over my dead body; they'll call him Clem"— and misspelled the Irish, orthographically odd Fintan, which translates, I was recently cheered to learn, as "white fire."

Trappist monks sharing evening meals with a pack of older siblings, with parents telling stories comfortably reaching back two centuries—this was a life that, knowing no other, I took for granted, even as it was not a life we saw acted out on television or in the movies or read about in books. Today, of the five surviving siblings, four, though married, live on or at the end of one-lane roads; each spends much or most of each day alone, gardening, working in wood, roaming the forest, painting and drawing, reading and writing. When in San Francisco, I live in Bernal Heights, the San Francisco equivalent of living at the end of a one-lane road.

I did not set out to be a solitary. In my twenties and thirties, I had a well-established pattern of serial monogamy, until in my mid-thirties I met the great love of my life, the only son of Holocaust survivors. He died of AIDS in a Paris hospital, a story I have written elsewhere, and though the grief was deep and enduring, I expected I would meet someone else and form another relationship, whether short-lived or lifelong. But years, then decades, passed with only an occasional date. Gradually I became aware that, though of course I knew periods of great loneliness, I also valued my solitude. Did

I really want a relationship? Or was I only responding to society's unceasing, ubiquitous message that to be complete, every human being requires a partner? Did it matter, in the end, whether my mid- and late-life solitude resulted from circumstance—so many gay men, arguably the best and brightest of my generation, were lost to AIDS that dating opportunities were few—or from the same aspect of my character that led my father to spend days living alone at the isolated cabin he built as a retreat, and my mother to insist on living alone well into her nineties?

Only recently, assisted by contemporary research on the role of birth order in shaping our destinies, have I come to realize how being the bookend of a large family is a special but fraught position. Farther back than I can recall, my mother and sisters taught me to read and write, but I cannot name any other skill, from riding a bicycle to managing finances, that I did not teach myself. I do not think of this history of benign neglect as a disadvantage. Laissez-faire parenting strikes me as preferable to helicopter parenting—but maybe that stance is only one more sign that I was born to solitude.

My mother was overwhelmed with the responsibility of cooking for ten-plus people daily, but she offered me a template for independence. While still a child she lost her mother and youngest sister, both of whom died at home, leaving her in charge of another younger sister and two younger brothers, with a father who was too preoccupied by keeping a roof over the heads of his ten surviving children to spare time for parenting. Like me, she raised herself. In her memoir *One Writer's Beginnings,* Eudora Welty writes, "It seems to me very likely that the element in my character that took possession of me on top of the mountain, the fierce independence that was suddenly mine, to remain inside me . . . was an inheritance. Indeed it was an inheritance from my mother . . . To grow up is to fight for it, to grow old is to lose it after having possessed it." When, in Welty's novella *The Robber Bridegroom*, Rosamund's father suggests that she submit to a tutor to learn Greek and to play the guitar, she cries, "Never! I will learn it all for myself," and in fact she does.

Both my mother's and my father's families had lived for many generations within a day's horseback ride of the Kentucky hills where their forebears settled. My mother's family arrived from beyond the Appalachians in the late 1700s, among the first settlers of what would later be named LaRue County. Their most famous neighbors were Thomas and Nancy Lincoln, who in 1809 gave birth to Abraham, their second child, on the nearby Sinking Spring Farm, before losing that property and relocating some ten miles north to Knob Creek, a six-mile-long tributary of the Rolling Fork River. Though today memorialized as a national monument, the precise location of the Lincolns' Knob Creek farm remains uncertain; it may well have been the same land that my father later rented from the distillery where he worked. What is certain is that Lincoln and his family drew water, worked, and played in the same small creek where, some 150 years later, my family drew water, worked, and played.

My father's family line most likely disappears into illegitimacy, though to conceal this stain the women of his family evolved fantastic stories involving nine brothers, with every brother except my great-grandfather killed in the Civil War. Then one of my sisters uncovered in the dusty files of the county courthouse a more plausible story, in which a part-Cherokee woman, Christina Richardson, is listed in the 1840 census as the mother of an illegitimate son, Thomas Hardin, born in 1835. In a lawsuit detailed in pages of flawlessly handwritten, seamless prose, the children of an elderly man named Alva

Johnson accuse Christina of having used her "devil woman's wiles" to seduce their father and secure a share of his estate. Then, as now, the law sided with blood over love; the judge overruled Alva's will and awarded Christina's share to his disgruntled relatives. Christina Richardson disappears from the town census along with her son Thomas Hardin—until 1870, when Thomas Hardin, born in 1835, reappears on the town rolls.

Now claiming Johnson as his last name (Christina's revenge?), this Thomas Hardin enrolled as a Union soldier in 1861. Kentucky was a border state that sent thousands of men to both sides of the Civil War; we have no clue as to why Thomas Hardin chose the Union. Given the race prejudice rampant during my childhood, I find it hard to imagine him as an abolitionist. More likely he was a federalist who believed in slavery—there it was, after all, enshrined in the Constitution—and maybe, as an impoverished illegitimate son, he licked the fingers of his fortune, held them to the wind, and sided with the cause that seemed most likely to emerge victorious. As an impoverished son with no prospects, he had little choice but to be pragmatic. Maybe Thomas Hardin's illegitimacy was the root of my various family members' affection for solitude—he who made his way without parents or siblings, in a world in which every relationship and transaction arose from clan connections.

Wounded in the arm at the battle of Stones River, Tennessee, on New Year's Day, 1863, Thomas Hardin was discharged from military service before the terrible final years of the war. He returned to the town of his birth and, using his Union pension, bought a rambling wood-frame hotel and renamed it the Sherwood Inn—again, for no reason that we can discern, though he must have known of the romantic tales of long-left-behind England and Scotland appropriated by the war-ravaged South. After that building burned in 1913, Patrick Dean, Thomas Hardin's oldest son and my grandfather, rebuilt it in brick and stone. He, or someone he hired, painted hunting scenes on the interior walls, with hills that look like those that cradle the town but with quail larger than the dogs who hunt them and dogs larger than their masters. My father, Patrick Dean, Jr., was born in 1910 in a white clapboard house behind the Sherwood. The Depression reduced the Sherwood to a tavern; with the end of rail passenger service and the arrival of the automobile, the hotel wing closed. That tavern, still owned by my family and now listed on the National Register of Historic Places, was one of the two most formative features of my childhood imagination. The second was the local Roman Catholic church.

Growing up, I was given to understand that the world was a constant place, that nothing would ever change, that my burning desire to get out, to flee my tiny village and vast family, to save my fundamentally bent self, was another of the many characteristics that defined me as an outlier. None of the men on my father's side had been educated beyond high school, a fact I offer without judgment. They remained in the town where they grew up, and the ring of low hills surrounding it defined their horizon. "You're too smart for your own good," my grade school nuns told me repeatedly. At the time I resented this comment—exactly how smart is too smart?—but after many years I came to a measure of understanding and, with it, forgiveness. My nuns were smart women born in the rural South, for whom the convent offered the only possibility of education, leading to no opportunities beyond teaching a large class of sullen, resentful, misbehaving children. "Too smart for your own good" was less a criticism than a warning born of experience.

I loved to read. This, I realized quickly, separated me from the rest of the boys as much as my bent sexuality. If there were other boys in town who liked to read, they knew well enough to conceal their affection, whereas I was too smitten to hide my love. (I am not much good at hiding anything, perhaps another characteristic of a solitary; my face so clearly reveals my heart that I might as well blurt my feelings out.) For my father, reading was a leisure activity, something undertaken at the end of a long day of hard labor. Though he regularly read a newspaper, he never grasped that a facility with language might be a way for someone to earn a living. College existed to train engineers; his sons would become engineers; his daughters would marry engineers; end of story. As a result, my sisters and I read on the sly, with a flashlight under the bedcovers or hiding behind an armchair, fearful that at any moment he would find us and sternly order us to get outside and do some real work. As with any love affair undertaken in secret, the subterfuge only increased its mystery and allure.

Before I went away to college, I had spent a great deal of time in the company of solitaries—the monks, vowed to solitude, and my parents, alone in their work spaces—but I had almost never experienced solitude. Youngest of nine children, a large family in a small town, who welcomed the first of many nieces and nephews when I was eight years old, I always knew there would be a line at the bathroom door. Supper commonly involved at least eight people, usually more, and usually guests. In town, in the general store, older folks would tilt up my chin and peer into my eyes. "I can tell you're a Johnson," they'd say, "but there's something else going on." My response—"My mother's a Hubbard. From Hodgenville"—brought a tightening of the lips and a nod. "Oh. Well. *Hodgenville.*" Ten miles away, but those were Protestant miles, and the Hodgenville gene pool was both unknown and suspect—though now, rounding the curve into the home stretch of life, I attribute my siblings' intelligence and creativity, as well as my lifelong philosophical conflicts, to that potent genetic conflation of tradition and rebellion, Roman Catholic and Protestant: mutts make the best dogs. Often I think it was that constant immersion in community that both led me to solitude but also gave me an experience of communal love—of love expressed not, as in conventional marriage, one on one, but in community, whether in a small town or among the monks.

In search of solitude I sometimes walked to the nearby river, the humble Rolling Fork, to sit on its bank, to contemplate its endless unrolling, its ongoing journey to the never-seen-but-often-imagined sea. I quickly learned to take along a cane fishing pole, not because I cared for fishing but because the pole provided a simulacrum of normalcy—when others stumbled upon me, it gave the unassailable excuse of *doing something useful*—though in fact all I wanted was to watch time and the river, alone.

Then I went away to college and heard people speak of hitch-hiking across Europe alone, or backpacking in the Sierras alone. Aloneness held a kind of mystery and allure; it struck me as a rite of passage, and in fact later I learned that many societies mark adulthood with a solitary journey away from the safety of family and community. Their example inspired my first foray into traveling alone: at nineteen years old, a train trip from Chamonix to Vienna, with an overnight stay in Zurich. Hardly the riskiest landscape, but I had no money and had no idea how one traveled—how, for example, to find and take a room in a hotel. That journey led to an adventure worthy of a Henry James short story, in which the leading Romansch poet of Switzerland, a man named Urs, whose opening gambit was "Do you like girls?," invited me to his Indian-print-draped apartment, where he put Leonard Cohen (a first for me) on the turntable and offered me hashish and did his best to get me into bed. I was as obdurately clueless as any James protagonist, less because I was ignorant of his desire than because I did not want to acknowledge it in myself. But that evening was the beginning of dismantling the lies I'd told myself—a first, tentative step toward self-knowledge. It would not have happened if I had not been traveling alone.

I tell this anecdote by way of encouraging every young person to hit the road alone, with a little less money in your wallet than your comfort zone allows. The world is hardly more dangerous today than it was for our immigrant forebears. Are we simply more afraid?

Within their marriage, my parents each created a sacred space—a place where they retreated in their individual search for the eternal in beauty. They'd never have spoken or claimed such a high-falutin phrase (I stole it from Zora Neale Hurston, with whom we will visit later in these pages), but they practiced that search every day of their lives. My mother retreated to her greenhouse (who, in 1950s' rural Kentucky, had a greenhouse?), where she cultivated orchids and cactus, the most exotic of flowers; my father went to his machine and woodworking shop—to us, his children, simply "the shop"—where he spent long hours making wood sculptures. As befits a sacred space, each place was a little intimidating—at least to me, the dreamer who preferred the world of books and ideas over the dirt of the greenhouse and the sawdust of the shop. Their particular smell is ever in my nose—the mildew and mold that hung out in the dark corners of the greenhouse, even through the hot months of summer, underlaid by the acrid chemical smell of the fertilizers and pesticides that my mother mercifully used sparingly but whose scent, with its polymerized bite, contrasted with the moist, earthy smell of dirt; and the shop's heady blend of the organic—wood shavings, dominated by sweet cedar, which my father favored for its insect-repellent properties but which evoked the smell of the incense used in church—with the industrial synthetics (paint, varnish, acetone, glue, gasoline) that he used liberally and that probably contributed to his death from cancer at seventy-four.

"Of a hundred ways to do something," my father said of me, "Fenton will choose the hardest." Many years later, I would be nonplussed to read, in Vincent van Gogh's sister-in-law's summary of Vincent's life, his father's assessment of his difficult son: "It seems as if he deliberately chooses the most difficult path." "To follow the paths trodden by others, to submit to the will of other people, that was not in his character, he wanted to work out his own salvation," van Gogh's sister-in-law wrote.

"To work out his own salvation"—those words, with all their philosophical and spiritual resonances, express what I have always felt to be true: that the greatest achievement in life is to work out the terms of one's own salvation, however one may define that term. "Free to make mistakes and be the master of one's own destiny," wrote Primo Levi of his life as a solitary in the years before his imprisonment in Auschwitz. Van Gogh sought to follow the words of the French philosopher Ernest Renan: "to sacrifice all personal desires, to realize great things, to obtain nobleness of mind, to surpass the vulgarity in which the existence of nearly all individuals is spent." These observations apply to most or all of the solitaries who, in their single-hearted dedication to their search, brought themselves to my attention.

It will be said: *These are the paths of genius, or the troubled, or both—but not paths for ordinary people.* But is not the most difficult path also the most rewarding? My father did not mean his observation ("Of a hundred ways, Fenton will choose the hardest") as a compliment. And yet he was a dreamer in his own right. I look back at his life and see that he, too, always chose the most difficult path. Surely, to offer only one example, it would have been easier to buy a house than, as he chose, to build one, then a second—his woodland retreat; but he was taking his place in a long tradition of solitaries building retreats. I do not know if my father had read Henry David Thoreau, but as Thoreau sheathed his Walden Pond cabin with boards recycled from an abandoned cottage (for which he paid $4.25), so my father recycled lumber salvaged from the distillery. In Thoreau he would have found a kindred spirit, as meticulous and exacting in his carpentry, since both found in wrack and ruin an inspiration to recycle and create.

From Thoreau's ten-by-fifteen-foot Walden Pond cabin and Cézanne's late-life studio Les Lauves in Provence to rural Kentucky, to the redwood deck of my father's HERMITage, the cabin he built with the help of his children and the monks in a century-old forest of beech trees—inconceivable to think of him as "Dad," this man whom everyone, related or not, called "Father," in this Catholic corner of the world where that particular honorific is reserved for priests. HERMITage was his own idiosyncratic spelling—he set it that way on two handsome signs he wood-burned with characteristic elegance and precision, one of which now hangs above the door to my home.

He who had spent so much time with monks set out in midlife to found a secular monastery. This was his plan: His friends would buy plots of land near the shores of Rough River Reservoir, among the first of the manmade lakes created by the Army Corps of Engineers in the watersheds of Kentucky. Each would build a woodland cabin, then after retiring they'd decamp en masse, emptying my tiny home town to take up residence in the woods, where they'd pass the days fishing and hunting and the nights drinking and telling stories about fishing and hunting. He persuaded some thirty men to join the nonprofit he created—the Rolling Fork Fish and Game Club—to broker the purchase of the land and then to buy lots laid out along the steep slopes of a ravine leading away from the newly-impounded lake.

As I visit the HERMITage in my imagination, I recall that, not long after my arrival as a college student in northern California, I proposed a secular collective to my friends, where we would spend our days reading and painting and gardening and our nights smoking pot and talking about reading and painting and gardening.

Of the men who bought lots, only Father saw his project through to completion. He was a self-taught builder and a dreamer, my father, a combination that led other men in other times to build the Taj Mahal, or the Panama Canal, or to write *In Search of Lost Time*. Under the influence of Brother Clement (born John Dorsey) and with the help of his Trappist friends, Father built a blue-collar version of

Fallingwater, the Frank Lloyd Wright–designed house cantilevered over a tumbling creek in the Pennsylvania forest.

He assembled the superstructure of the HERMITage from left-overs from monastery construction projects, using surplus steel to build a deck that projected into the canopies of the surrounding beech trees. Several of the monks volunteered welding and wiring skills, and he had the more-and-less enthusiastic help of his children, but as the monks left the enclosure to reenter the secular world and his children grew into our lives, he began working more and more alone.

You must understand, this place was *remote*. The nearest towns, each with a few hundred inhabitants, were almost twenty winding miles distant. The closest legal alcohol was a seventy-mile drive (Father took care to pack his own). In the days of the construction of the HERMITage, from the paved state highway we drove six or seven miles along a gravel road, then turned onto a rutted track that led to land owned by Dempster and Leela Kiper, country folks for whom a trip to the county seat was a once-a-year odyssey under-taken with unease and trembling. When we first arrived, they lived in a shack with an outhouse weather-beaten to the color of the mice with whom they shared quarters. Some years later that shack burned, and my father assembled his Trappist friends to build a three-room replacement, painted pale yellow and with indoor plumbing, a palace the likes of which had never entered the Kipers' imaginations. How I wish I'd been there to watch them enter it for the first time!

Dempster was small and skinny and wrinkled as a prune, while the much younger Leela was a vast roiling mound of flesh, snaggle-toothed and ever in good cheer—Jack Sprat and his wife. My father was a prince from a distant land, impossibly wealthy in their eyes, but he had more in common with them than with the swells and he was seldom so happy as when sitting on the porch of the tiny home he had caused to be built, with Dempster accepting slugs of whiskey from Father's flask and Leela—"Little," to my father—spreading wide her ample thighs to air her privates to the humid summer air.

When I write that the Kipers always seemed content, I am not romanticizing or—Lord knows—envying their hardscrabble life, but merely offering what I observed to be true. They were among a cast of solitaries who, courtesy of my father's respect for and emulation of their independent ways, populated my family's life. Now I know that they were a vanishing breed—people for whom subsistence living was a way of life, who came by their protein from the business end of a shotgun or fishing pole rather than from a grocery store; people who were solitaries in their assumption of self-sufficiency.

And then down into the holler. After carting in building materials—among them a large copper water storage tank salvaged from the now-closed distillery and fed from a spring through an elaborate network of pipes—Father allowed the forest to reclaim the primitive road, so that the only access to the HERMITage was down a narrow trail that snaked along a creek before dropping over a sixty-foot limestone cliff. The front of the cabin was double-paned glass, so that the solitary lived in a universe of chlorophyll, at one with the temperate jungles of the South—beech and white oak and hickory and dogwood and poplar and the great oval palmate leaves of cucumber magnolia, with poison ivy rampant. The place is locally famous for an ash tree that my father left to grow up through a hole in its deck. "Ain't that the place with the tree growing through it?" locals would say, in tones that convey that they know what my father knew but did not plan for, which is that over time trees get bigger. The sapling that once barely cleared the deck grew to seventy feet tall, its trunk filling the hole cut to accommodate it. The tree was too tall to top and too large to cut down and each time we returned accompanied by dread that in our absence a wind would have taken down the tree and with it much of the cabin.

Seeking to repair the ravine bank disturbed in the construction, my mother brought in snippets of English ivy, which turned into a temperate forest kudzu, swallowing first trees, then boulders, then the cabin itself—an environmental catastrophe, as she sorrowfully conceded. Humans draw mice, mice draw snakes, so before long the ivy became home to a host of reptiles, some of them poisonous. "Do not kill snakes—they are our friends," Father wrote in his instructions for visitors, but the interior walls were festooned with the skins of any number of friends he had killed and gutted and stretched on cedar planks.

As he aged he lived there alone, longer and longer. Once, while he was working alone, a plank fell sixty feet from the cliff, splitting open his forehead. He patched the wound with duct tape and rags splashed with kerosene for disinfectant and kept on working. He lived there for days in which he would not have spoken with a living soul—Cézanne had nothing on him. By day the forest was a symphony of birdsong. By night the place was creepy for anyone of suburban sensibilities—intensely alive with the grindings and chatterings of the insects of the Southern forest as well as the squeaks and howls and hoots of the nocturnal hunters—owl and raccoon, fox and possum and the ghosts the imagination conjures in the dark, ghosts of my father and his companion monks.

The place has served as a trysting spot for any number of family lovers and surely for lovers of whom we're unaware. Among these were my now-deceased partner and me, in one of the happiest moments of our time together. Child of Los Angeles and Europe, he had never experienced any place so wild. He bore a bee sting like a badge of courage.

I have spent time in solitude at the HERMITage, partly by way of seeking the spirit and guidance of the dead. One humid summer evening I sat on the deck as darkness fell, trying to conjure up my partner's ghost or that of my father. Neither appeared, but in the next morning's dawn light, as I sat in the same place looking over the ravine to the magnificent, mottle-barked beeches, I was startled by the utterly silent flight of a great horned owl returning from its nighttime hunt. Its noiseless descent through the dense forest gave form and flesh to silence.

"My knowledge of myself in silence . . . which is beyond words and concepts because it is utterly particular . . . opens out into the silence of God," writes Thomas Merton. Words and concepts identify our shared realities, but silence is the language of the self, of each person's particular reality, and so only in silence may I come to know myself. And so, though the Spirit dwells in all things and all people, we come really to know her only in solitude and in silence.

From Merton's hermitage at the Abbey of Gethsemani, a meadow slopes southward to a gap in the forest, framing a pastoral view of fields and farms, rolling to the long blue line of Muldraugh's Hill— the same view today, if now partly obscured by trees, that Merton saw in 1965 when, after years of petitioning his abbot, he moved into this hermitage, built with the help of the same monks who were simultaneously helping my father build his HERMITage at Rough River.

Three years after Merton occupied it, he would be dead. Today a cell phone tower rises in the center of this bucolic landscape, topped by a flashing red semaphore that blinks off and on through the night. The tower carries all the predictable resonances—intrusion of the contemporary, technology-obsessed world into this space of meditation, omnipresence of Big Brother—with the additional irony that it was built in part in response to complaints from visitors who come to the abbey on silent retreats only to find that, left alone with their consciences, they reach for their phones.

On this humid August afternoon I am sitting on the porch with my poet monk friend Paul Quenon and a retired community college English teacher, who is thus by definition a saint. Paul, who is in his seventies and who memorizes poetry as a way of keeping his mind active, eggs us on to recite memorized lines.

The retired teacher recites from Whitman's *Leaves of Grass*:

> I think I could turn and live with animals, they are so
>   placid and self-contained,
> I stand and look at them long and long.
> They do not sweat and whine about their condition,
> They do not lie awake in the dark and weep for their sins,
> They do not make me sick discussing their duty to God,
> Not one is dissatisfied, not one is demented with the mania
>   of owning things,
> Not one kneels to another, nor to his kind that lived
>   thousands of years ago,
> Not one is respectable or unhappy over the whole earth.

Paul recites one of his poems:

When I write my last poem
it will not say good-by
to poetry, but hello to itself,

will heave a glad sigh
it got into the world
before the door closed,

will look to its companion poems,
that it might have place
among these orphans,

that they might reach out hands
in company to go together
into oblivion or into memory,

or to some secret cove
where eternity sits,
from time to time, and reads.

Then evening gathers on the lush green meadow that slopes away from the hermitage to a dark line of forest and the distant, lumpy profile of my beloved Knobs, with the red semaphore atop the cell tower blinking on, off, on, off, presence, absence, presence, absence. I bask in this lovely stream of words, this tour de force of memorization, thinking: *This is why one becomes a monk: to cultivate in every moment presence to the beauty of the world.*

And then my turn comes. Inspired by Paul, I have taken up memorizing poetry, a practice I recommend. Print a poem and tape it to the dashboard of your car, or to your bathroom mirror, and with minimal and pleasurable labor, in a week or two you'll have constructed a refuge available when you're stalled in traffic, or stuck on the subway, or naked and shivering and alone on the gurney as the massive, radiation-emitting machine whirrs and clicks around your body. This evening I recite Marianne Moore's "What Are Years":

> . . . satisfaction is a lowly
> thing, how pure a thing is joy.

I have not told my friends that I am writing about solitude, but sitting on Merton's porch, each of us chose to recite poems by solitaries.

Perhaps this coincidence, if it is that, owes itself to Merton and his persistence in obtaining permission to build his hermitage. Thanks to Brother Paul, I have sat on its porch many times, in all seasons and all weathers, and the experience is always magical. With rare exceptions the guests are, if not themselves solitaries, at least unaccompanied by their spouses.

That's what I'm trying to tell you. Some of us are called to marry, but even those called to marriage will enrich their lives and their marriages by making time for solitude, for experiencing themselves alone so as to bring that self, refreshed and renewed, back into relationship; and even those who are married will benefit from spending time alone with solitaries. The measure in which your solitude is hard is the measure of the reward it offers.

◌

My father's HERMITage fell into disrepair. The ravine, with its steep sides and relentless humidity, was poorly suited for building. The site is located to the south and west of the region's population centers (Louisville, Cincinnati), whose opportunities drew the children and grandchildren north and east, so that the cabin is more remote than ever from anyone who might care for it. Root by root, tendril by tendril, the English ivy meticulously separated the chimney from its foundation. Years of ice storms toppled trees over the power line. The access road has long disappeared, the access path eroded. The redwood deck rotted and is no longer safe to bear weight. The steep rise in the price of copper occasioned the theft of the massive spring-fed holding tank, reservoir for the water supply. Vandals have broken the locks and entered, torn open the walls to strip the copper wires, torn out the ancient refrigerator's motor for its copper parts. Today I received the report that my brothers sold the HERMITage to someone we suspect to have been among the vandals.

In my early teens, after the nightly news—which my father and I watched regularly, alone together—after yet another gruesome horror of the 1960s, a napalm bombing or assassination or riot, I made some bitter comment. My father, not a patient man, lost his composure. "I whip your brothers and they stand there and take it and then they do what I tell them," he said. "I whip you and you cry and then you do whatever you were going to do anyway. Why can't you be like them?" A spirit at my ear told me what to say and so I said it. "Because I'm so much like you." A stunned silence followed, in which we both understood that I had spoken the truth.

He longed, I think, to understand what power books held, that they would lead his son to throw away a fantastic opportunity—an engineering degree—in hopes of one day writing them. Sometime after I went away to Stanford, on a scholarship underwritten by Seagram, he must have heard me say how much William Faulkner's writing meant to me; in my junior year I returned home to find my battered copy of Faulkner's *Absalom, Absalom!* on his nightstand. I never asked, he never volunteered what he thought of this challenging novel about a smart kid from the South who flees to Harvard, where he is unable to reconcile his Southern roots with the racism and bigotry from which they are inextricable, a contradiction that drives him to suicide.

I did not commit suicide, though I came close, because I found refuge in San Francisco, in those days a city of misfits and solitaries who comforted and cared for one another, because in those days each one of us bent people had known loneliness in the most intimate way and, having known such hunger, understood why and how we needed to support one another in our solitude. Each of us knew, to adapt the words of Emily Dickinson, what it meant to starve of little love.

My father was a dreamer, yes, but he built his dream. That his friends were less visionary or more pragmatic is, I realize in retrospect, to be expected. Ought he to have devoted his time instead to, say, parenting his younger children, whom he left fatherless while he worked on his HERMITage? He is hardly the first artist and solitary to make that choice. Long after his death, I, his youngest child, face the choice of resenting his obsession or being grateful for having known, however distantly, a man who had a dream and built it.

"[U]ntil we have begun to fail we have no way of working out our success," Merton writes. Sitting in silence, I am working out in words what my father worked out in brick and cement and steel. Was the HERMITage a failure? For sure, my father's plan of a secular monastic community did not come to pass. Built of steel tubing and steel panel walls, the building's superstructure will endure for centuries, even as its bricks and wood are digested by English ivy as thoroughly as liana swallowed the great Mayan temples.

> After my father died, I came to my home in Kentucky and realized I was my father.
>
> James Still

My father began serious work on his HERMITage in 1966, when he was fifty-six years old—the age at which I began this book.

CHAPTER 3

I to Myself

Henry David Thoreau

THAT WE ALTERNATELY TRASH or idolize our solitaries suggests something about our need for idols elsewhere in our lives; but, as the Buddha and Hebrew biblical prophets point out repeatedly, idols are an avoidance mechanism, a place where we can park and abandon our dreams instead of accepting our responsibility to live them out— to actualize them, to incarnate them through our lives. The vocalist Nina Simone railed against this phenomenon: audiences who paid to witness her anger and heartbreak on stage and then left the theater to go about their lives unchanged. What these solitaries do is so hard—or such is the commonplace myth—so eccentric and daunting that ordinary people couldn't possibly achieve it, and so the solitary must either be surpassingly strange or possess some unique strength or both. In fact, as reading Henry David Thoreau makes uncomfortably clear, all that's required is to pull out our ear buds and turn off our camera phones and listen to the sounds, pleasant and troubling alike, that the universe provides, including most especially its silence.

The notion of Thoreau as a hermit is so far from the facts that what's curious is why it developed in the first place, since *Walden* is

replete with anecdotes of chatty visits from townspeople and travelers and lengthy passages praising the virtues of simple hospitality
("You need not rest your reputation on the dinners you give"). Far
from being a wilderness, Walden Pond was an easy walk from the
center of Concord and a regular destination for picnics and anglers,
a fact Thoreau never conceals because he is writing, not to manufac-
ture a myth but to craft a good sentence. "No other male American
writer," observes Laura Dassow Wilds in her fine and sympathetic
biography, "has been so discredited for enjoying a meal with loved
ones or for not doing his own laundry." The reasons for that dis-
crediting, I argue, arise from our need to savage solitaries who so
emphatically and cheerfully break social norms, because they show
how easily it may be done, as well as our suspicion and mistrust of
those who sing in praise of solitude. We seem either to mock (Thoreau) or idolize (Thomas Merton) those who seek and enjoy solitude,
perhaps because perceiving them as ordinary folks might require
us to question the cocoon of noise and artificial light with which we
surround ourselves and that constitutes contemporary life. Critics
demean Thoreau for allowing Ralph Waldo Emerson, dean of New
England writers and Thoreau's advocate and benefactor, to pay his
poll tax to spring him from the night in jail that resulted in "Civil
Disobedience," Thoreau's most famous essay—but those same critics overlook that Thoreau risked much graver penalties when he
assisted slaves fleeing to Canada, since the Fugitive Slave Act of 1850
imposed significant fines and up to six months in prison for anyone
caught helping runaways.

     In *Walden* and elsewhere, Thoreau wrote a prose oratorio in
praise of solitude, and let his readers pause in due reverence: the
man sure knew how to turn a phrase. I am not surprised to learn

that the book required four times as long to write as he spent living on the pond—eight drafts in ten years. The writing bears witness to that slow and patient hand. Out of print at the time of Thoreau's death, *Walden* has since taken on a life of its own, packed as it is with aphorisms that have entered the common parlance of many who have no idea of their origin: "The mass of men lead lives of quiet desperation." "My greatest skill has been to want but little." (My version, arrived at independently: "The secret to contentment is low overhead.") "If a man loses pace with his companions, perhaps it is because he hears a different drummer. Let him step to the music which he hears, however measured, or far away," this last so familiar as to be enshrined in an Internet source called ClichéWeb. "Men have become tools of their tools."

Any one of those pithy sentences—and *Walden* and his voluminous other writings contain many more—could serve as a koan for a Buddhist monk, but I do Thoreau a disservice if I pigeonhole him as an aphorist. His writing teaches us to slow down and look at the world. "No method or discipline can supersede the necessity of being forever on the alert," he writes, Buddhism summarized in a sentence. "What is a course of history, or philosophy, or poetry . . . compared to the discipline of looking always at what is to be seen?" He finds as much to see and remark upon in a road cut or a farm pond as other writers find in the Himalayas.

Thoreau is the prophet of empiricism, showing us through his writing how the road cut and the farm pond are imbued with the divine—in the same manner as Cézanne, who sought to paint the soul in a sugar bowl. In place of angels, Thoreau has birds; for his visions of God, he turns to the pine and the rock. His descriptions of his encounters with the natural world match the writing of any mystic regarding an encounter with the Divine. "The earth is all alive and covered with papillae. The largest pond is as sensitive to atmospheric changes as the globule of mercury in its tube." Melting ice is the "blood of winter." "[T]here is nothing inorganic . . . the earth . . . is living poetry like the leaves of a tree."

He writes "living poetry" in the form of prose, celebrating the interior journey. "We are for the most part more lonely when we go abroad among men than when we stay in our chambers," he writes. "God is alone,—but the devil, he is far from being alone; he sees a great deal of company; he is legion." To write as much is to underscore what psychologists tell us: every partner to relationship, every single parent raising children, every caregiver, needs time alone, down time in which to relocate the beat of her or his own drum, because in that unique beat lies our particular access to the rhythms of love. Without time deliberately dedicated to solitude, partnership, parenting, and caregiving become rote, and it is a short step from rote to abuse.

So what *is* solitude? Asked to define it, most would describe the simple fact—difficult or impossible for many of us to bear for long—of being alone. But clearly Thoreau has something else in mind: "Solitude is not measured by the miles of space that intervene between a man and his fellows."

As critic Harold Bloom has pointed out, the interior journey lies at the heart of the American national identity. It differentiates even American Roman Catholics—who among U.S. churchgoers retain the most direct spiritual connection to their European roots—from Roman Catholics elsewhere in the world. Pope John XXIII might have espoused the doctrine of the primacy of the individual conscience, but, among Roman Catholics, Americans observe it most enthusiastically. "I never had much use for authority," my mother declared, epitomizing in a sentence why Americans are such a headache for popes and prelates. She was a convert from Bible Belt Protestantism and as such had no truck with being told what to believe, but in the United States even cradle Catholics grow up in a Protestant land and so absorb via osmosis an interest in shaping for and by ourselves the terms of our encounter with the sacred.

Emerson eloquently articulated this essential American characteristic—the search for a personal, particular spiritual philosophy not without but within—in his essay "Self-Reliance," but Bloom traces its appearance and role in every major American religious, spiritual, or philosophic practice. It fueled the fervor of the first great revivals at Cane Ridge in Kentucky in 1801 and in the "burned-over district" of the early 1800s in upstate New York, where it gave birth to Mormonism. It explains our current fascination with Asian philosophies, introduced into American thinking by Emerson and by Thoreau, whom Emerson commissioned to translate the *Bhagavad-Gita* and who wrote that he preferred it over all other wisdom writings. "Everywhere I use 'God,'" Emerson wrote in a letter, "I would prefer to use 'Budh'"—his spelling of our contemporary "Buddha"— but even he, who challenged the Harvard Divinity School with his unorthodox beliefs, was not willing to risk his reputation and livelihood by publicly rejecting the Christian personification of an omnipotent and omniscient power.

In keeping with their times, my parents were reserved. I never saw my father touch my mother in public, even to hold hands. Neither parent told me that she or he loved me until late in life, long after my father's death, when, after many trips to California, my mother grew more comfortable with speaking, in addition to showing, what she felt. But I grew up with the assumption, woven into the fabric of my consciousness, of security. Somehow my parents, for whom money was scarce, would always provide. There was the land—a huge vegetable garden—and the river, whose fish were free for the taking, and the woods and fields, with their supply of small game and deer, and there was the understanding, commonplace among those who have little, that we had a responsibility to help one another. From ambition or anger or in investigation of my solitude I might leave home, but that inbred understanding of the importance and necessity of collective endeavor would never leave me.

At the same time, I understood that, when I became an adult, I had a destiny uniquely my own, not to be dictated by distant authorities, whether in Washington, New York, or Rome, which it was my responsibility to seize and shape. I would receive no financial support because there was none to be given. This was a great advantage—not materially, of course, but creatively and spiritually. My parents each had a rich interior life, and they brought those lives to their communities; they left their community, my small town, a better place. Using books loaned by the monks, my mother founded a library in an abandoned gas station; today it occupies a handsome building that would be the pride of any town. My father was not a joiner—he was, of the pair, the more dedicated solitary—but he donated money and skills to community groups. They were solitaries living their lives not codependent but in parallel. Theirs was, I believe, a healthy marriage.

The distillery where my father oversaw maintenance made a bourbon called Antique, and practiced small-batch distilling before the marketers named the practice. My father was proud of his product in an unassuming way—a way rooted in his character, which, in our flash-and-dazzle-over-pause-and-think world, knew only one way to accomplish a task, any task, no matter how trivial, and that was to put all his heart and soul into it. He would have scorned the concept of multitasking, since to do several tasks at once was inevitably to short-change them all. In this he was a kind of Zen master.

But I have gotten ahead of the story of the virgin cypress.

In the 1930s, after the end of Prohibition, Seagram bought and expanded a small-batch distillery which dated from the 1800s. It added vast, deep tubs to hold and heat the mixture of ground corn and grains, water and sugar and yeast, cooked and then distilled to produce alcohol, a byproduct of fermentation that might be thought of as yeast poop. A favorite trick of my father's was to take an unsuspecting guest on a distillery tour, in the course of which he would open a small window in the cover of the steaming vat of mash and invite the visitor to take a deep breath. *That* would knock you off your feet.

The vats were made of old-growth cypress, a tree that roots itself in swamps and thus possesses a hard, fine grain nearly impervious to water and wear. The vats were cleaned after every use with scalding water. I recall a story, probably true, of a laborer parboiled when he was mistakenly shut into a tub during the cleaning process. In any case, the clank and roar and rumble and stink of the distillery frightened me, a timid child, or perhaps a sensible child who even then did not share my father's indifference to occupational hazards. When my father took me on a tour I dragged my feet, providing the first evidence that this, his youngest and book-brightest child, was not going to pursue a career as an engineer.

Sometime in the 1950s Seagram shifted to stainless steel vats, presumably because of their ease of cleaning and because, no matter how impervious, the cypress tubs were showing the effects of years of being filled with witches' hot brew. As the cypress was removed, plank by plank, my father stored it to one side of the distillery workshop. Under his hand, those cypress planks from the distillery mash tubs became tongue-and-groove paneling for the interior of his new house. For the first decade after my family moved in, the house reeked of bourbon mash; for another ten years, a visitor could evoke a life now gone by pressing her nose to the grooves in the paneling and taking a deep breath.

One of my first childhood memories is following my father into his shop—another place of dust and whine and roar—to watch as he guided the cypress boards through the planer, a fantastically dangerous machine lacking, of course, any cautions or protections. The planer peeled away the top, mash-permeated layer of cypress to reveal the cream-white grain underneath. A waist-high device with a roller bar and a heavy metal base embossed with the Coca-Cola trademark supported the long planks as they came out of the planer, but the longest of the planks required the support of a guiding hand so as to be kept level and prevent the weight of the plank from pinching the planer blade. At times when no one else was at hand, Father called me to the job. I was barely tall or strong enough to support the plank's heavy weight and lived in terror that I was going to let it slip and incur my father's disdain or, even worse, wrath. His disdain I learned to live with, but you did not want to incur his wrath.

Years later, when I told the story of the cypress planks to a fellow student in college, he exclaimed, "Why, that was nothing but theft!" Child of corporate suburbia, he did not realize that in the 1950s, had my father not claimed the mash-permeated cypress that we now see as priceless, it would have rotted in an open dump. Nor did he understand the underground economies of strapped rural communities, which—until the arrival of plastic and an economy of disposables—practiced recycling long before it became hip in urban enclaves. Had my father thought that cypress had a future other than the dump, he'd have left it to that future. Or so I like to think.

At the new house, now under construction, my father and his older sons laid the planed cypress planks on a great block of limestone, which served as a staging area for every family activity from major construction projects to cleaning fish—one end of the block had a cylindrical hole through which blood and guts could drain into a pan for the ever-present dogs. The block was about seven feet long, three feet wide, and two feet deep—when I cited these figures in front of an audience, an engineer pulled out his phone and, working from the average density of limestone, calculated the rock's weight: somewhere between 5,000 and 7,000 pounds. The stone had been used as a hitching block for the teams of great draft horses that before modernization had pulled loads of grain to the distillery. Draft horses are bred for size and strength, and the hitching post to which they were tied needed serious gravity so as to hold them if they spooked. Five to seven thousand pounds of limestone met the requirement. The cylindrical hole had once enclosed a brass pole, to which the horses' reins had been tied.

How that block got three miles from the distillery to my parents' new house is a mystery, though the distillery had block-and-tackle and my father had determination and sons, and thus the pyramids got built. Once the stone reached our house, my father lowered it (from what? how?) onto four old-style car jacks, one at each corner, which sat on a cement pad that had been poured to support the stone's weight. To build the stone table's legs, each jack raised the stone a notch, a crowbar was inserted, and one of my brothers risked life or at least permanent dismemberment by sliding in a thin flagstone slab slathered with cement. No, that can't be true. Surely the flagstone legs were constructed first, then the block lowered onto them? Either way, in the end a three-ton, flagstone-legged table was created—a table that will mystify archeologists a thousand years hence, when the house and all around it have long disappeared. What exotic rites were performed here? For what god or goddess was this altar built?

Next to the limestone table, an enormous brass kettle—another theft from the distillery?—hung suspended from a tripod welded by one of the monks. These were the years of modernization, the 1950s, when everything new was presumed to be an improvement on what had come before. The distillery was replacing old tools and materials, leaving them free for the taking. The kettle we used for making burgoo.

Now, burgoo. Decades later I was contacted by the Kitchen Sisters from National Public Radio, asking for a recipe for this peculiarly Kentucky dish. "Well," I said, "you start with wild game—"

The host interrupted. "Wild game? Everyone else I've talked to says chicken or pork."

"Everyone else grew up in the suburbs," I retorted. "The defining ingredient for burgoo is wild game—little animals, squirrel and quail and rabbit, thrown into the stew to give it that gamey taste. You can't call it burgoo unless the base is wild game. Otherwise you're just making plain old stew."

Burgoo was the meal of choice for winter parties. Every man brought his wild game—though there was hen and pork and goat for good measure—and tossed it into the pot, along with tomatoes canned from the previous summer's gardens, potatoes, carrots, and whatever leftovers the wives' refrigerators or fruit cellars yielded, with slugs of bourbon thrown in to make a down-home marinade. The stew was cooked overnight, or at least all day, over an open fire, while the town residents slid down the nearby hill, using abandoned car hoods for sleds. After the snow had been packed into a sheet of ice, these slabs of metal developed great speed, and a common trick was to pile onto the five or six people already on board as the hood sped by. The car hoods had razor-sharp edges and the undertaking was great fun and fantastically dangerous, as proved to be the case when someone was gravely injured by a hood slicing open his leg. That put an end to that particular party, though I close my eyes and smell the smoke from the fire, the gamey-scented, mouthwatering burgoo, and see the shadows the fire's flickering light casts on the cross-hatching of the tree trunks and limbs against the darkening winter sky, with scarlet spattered across the snowdrifts . . . and there we are, dark figures against the white snow, muffled against the cold, preserved for as long as memory and paper endure.

"What is religion?" Thoreau wrote in his journal, and immediately supplied the answer: "That which is never spoken." One might offer the same observation about genuine love, or—as Thoreau wrote in a different context—reverence. Metaphor, parable, symbol, allegory— these ways of telling the truth slantwise provide our best means of accessing religion; these, and silence, and solitude.

So it is that our fact-obsessed age loses sight of truth. Administrations at big public universities increasingly pressure their faculties to measure students by their knowledge of facts, when what they need—what in my classes they ask for—is an education in truth. "They who know no purer sources of truth . . . stand, and wisely stand, by the Bible and the Constitution, and drink at it there with reverence and humanity," Thoreau wrote. "But they who behold where it comes trickling into this lake or that pool, gird up their loins once more, and continue their pilgrimage toward its fountainhead." Seek the source, Thoreau urges us—the foundation on which we have built our society, which some call love and some call God and some are wise enough not to name at all. And the clear implication underlying Thoreau's directive is that this ultimate source of wisdom must be sought in silence and in solitude.

Thoreau attracts me—he continues to fascinate, because in our materialist age he offers a model for cheerfully and exuberantly living a life of poverty and chastity, without, so far as I can determine, having taken formal vows; though through his life and his writing Thoreau teaches us to reject the words "poverty" and "chastity," with their negative connotations. What human being has exceeded Thoreau's wealth? Who has given and received more love? I think of him as a secular monk, living a life of simplicity and right conduct—a gentler and more accurate description of his choices.

But what of obedience, the third of the traditional monastic vows that include poverty and chastity? Indeed, Thoreau practiced the hardest form of obedience—that is, obedience to his conscience. He educated himself in the contemporary manifestations of human injustice and, within the bounds of the practicable, he removed himself from their machinery. I consider the monastic vows (poverty,

chastity, obedience) in this context because Thoreau serves so well
as a model for a contemporary secular asceticism.

Some time in the 1990s, my mother and I were driving past the
great edifice of Merton's Abbey of Gethsemani. My mother gestured
at the walls. "Not in my lifetime but in yours," she said, "you'll drive
past this place and say, 'There used to be a monastery here.'" Fewer
than forty monks remain at Gethsemani, down from a peak of well
over two hundred in Merton's day, and the average age is pushing
seventy-five. Impossible for me to imagine that this institution, near
which I grew up and which I still visit, will not be a fixture of my
life—but soon enough, barring an uptick in monastic vocations, I
may not have to imagine its absence.

But does ascetic practice require bricks and mortar? Did the
disappearance of the culture that enabled and financed the building
of the great medieval monasteries at Cluny or La Grande Chartreuse
or Cîteaux or, in America, at Gethsemani mean the disappearance
of the virtues they were intended to cultivate and inspire? Might
contemplative traditions endure without bricks-and-mortar institutions where one may retreat from time to time in search of silence
and beauty? Might the current interest in contemplative practice—
meditation, yoga, centering prayer, solitude—lead to a society in
which reverence, not irony, is the dominant mode? I am always
conscious that many of the greatest saints of my admiration and
acquaintance never darken the doors of a church—though Thoreau
gave lectures in church basements, and was, not surprisingly, a great
enthusiast for meditation.

The demise of monasticism has been predicted many times, and
yet the impulse to contemplation—to a simple life—the impulse that

led to the founding of monasteries, seems always to survive. But the model for a contemplative life of the future may be less the grand edifices of Europe, however impressive they are, or the grand edifice of the Abbey of Gethsemani, but the individual who quietly pursues a solitary contemplative practice in the privacy of her home, meeting occasionally with a small group of like-minded spirits dedicated to changing the world not through revolution but through mindfulness and compassion. In this I am comfortable with situating Thoreau among our panoply of solitary, secular American saints.

CHAPTER 4

The Psychology of the Earth

Paul Cézanne

MARSEILLE WAS FOUNDED BY Greeks, Aix by Romans, "which explains everything," said the guide at Les Lauves, the studio of Paul Cézanne, located just north of Aix-en-Provence. The "everything" that is thus explained was, I assumed, the contrast between the cheerful chaos and grime of Marseille and well-scrubbed, bourgeois Aix.

On a bright blue November day I'd taken lunch in one of the squares of Aix, after which I visited its fine tapestry museum, wandering among beautiful objects created by anonymous weavers who found meaning in refining the skills of their hands, in their daily encounter with learning from and shaping the material world, in pride in their unsigned work. Years later, a less enraptured friend tells me the weavers worked in terrible conditions that ruined their vision and that they contracted diseases from poisons in their dyes . . . and no doubt she was right, but their work was no more debilitating than assembling microchips, and they, at least, lived and died for beauty.

When I emerged from the tapestry museum the sky was a lowering sheet of gray, but I hiked up the road to Cézanne's studio anyway, remembering my dictum: *Never change your plans because of the weather, be Zen and go with the weather, let the weather reveal itself to you in all its variety and grandeur.* Halfway to the studio I began to see little snowflakes, and by the time I arrived at Les Lauves, Cézanne's studio, flurries were falling.

I strolled in the lovely, unkempt garden, then went inside, the only visitor, so the guides were chatty and told me how Cézanne used funds inherited on his mother's death to hire an architect to design this big, nicely proportioned late nineteenth-century French residence, with a large painting studio incorporated into the second floor with a huge window to the north for indirect light and two smaller windows to the south so that he could have southern light when he wanted. In fact, the story of the house is more complicated, but in that particular moment I was content to listen to mellifluous French evoking Cézanne leaning on his contractor to get it done, get it done, he was sixty-three and had so much work he wanted to do. The house was finished in nine months. Four years later, in October of his sixty-seventh year, on one of his frequent expeditions to Mont Sainte-Victoire, though a cold autumn rain was falling, he continued painting (*never change your plans because of the weather, be Zen and go with the weather*). There he caught pneumonia; a few days later he died.

I gravitated to Cézanne the first time I set foot in a museum, eighteen years old, in France at a university overseas program not in order to learn French but to escape being drafted into the Vietnam War. I would require decades living in large cities before I understood why he drew me so powerfully. Like me, he was a country boy and a draft resister. Like another of my favorites, his fourteenth-century brother-in-painting Giotto, whose sculptural forms Cézanne's figures evoke, Cézanne rooted his life and his work equally in faith and reason and saw no contradiction between them. I look at his paintings and understand that this is a man who grew up as I grew up—carrying the Virgin through the streets in May, swimming in the river in July, speaking a rough-hewn country idiom, probably told that he was "too smart for his own good," hearing the old stories of gods and goddesses and saints and emerging from the classroom to search for them in the forests and fields and hills, because that was where their spirits lived and because, bluntly put, that was the whole of his world, the only world he knew. He would have to find the gods and goddesses and saints here or find them nowhere.

In Cézanne's painting, the sacred becomes flesh and dwells among us. Long before contemporary quantum physics, Cézanne understood that all moments are present to this moment. (No, really, they are. Albert Einstein: "This distinction between past, present, and future is an illusion, however tenacious.") Gertrude Stein described the key to Cézanne's revolution: the realization that "in composition one thing was as important as another thing. Each part is as important as the whole"—an observation that also describes the philosophical and ecological revolution of the twentieth century, with Cézanne's fractured landscapes among the forces that set it in motion. American and Western European thinkers began the twentieth century as specialists, teasing out each strand from the whole for intensive study. We ended it at the threshold of understanding that everything is interconnected; that there is no separation between any object or creature and its environment; that any separation does some violence to the phenomenon being studied; that there is no separation between self and other; that the universe is not linear, proceeding in a tidy chronological line from point A to point B, but a continuing process, an unending becoming. The novelist George Sand quoted Cézanne's mentor, the painter and fellow solitary Eugène Delacroix, saying, "Neither the light that strikes this contour nor the shadow that glides lightly over it have a seizable stopping point"—that is, despite our illusions to the contrary, there is no border or boundary between the object and the light that strikes it, between the object and its surroundings, between now and past or future, between you and me, between us and the universe. In embracing this fact of the interconnectedness of all being, we are their students.

Cézanne began his artistic life as a poet and translator before shifting to painting, and was a voracious and discriminating reader—possibly the best-read painter of his day. Like almost all European artists of the time, he was deeply influenced by *le japonisme*, the flood of Asian art and philosophy that inundated Europe after Commodore Perry forcibly opened Tokyo harbor to the world in 1853. Asian art revealed to nineteenth-century European painters a vast new range of possibilities of the brush. The excitement and power of Cézanne's painting arises from the coupling of the warm, earthy sensuality of his native Roman Catholicism, tinged in the south of France with heretic and pre-Roman, animist roots, with the precise, cool contemplation espoused by the Buddhist, Asian ideal of communion with nature.

Melancholics, among whom later in his life Cézanne counted himself, need less a particular friend, much less a spouse, than the presence of friendship as the foundation for their creativity. Here, too, the pattern of his life matches mine. Cézanne's life was characterized by deep, intense friendships with men whom he left behind when the currents of life and work carried him elsewhere but who remained fully present and influential in his heart.

At thirteen he formed his most significant relationship with another person, equal in consequence to his marriage or his fatherhood and in passion second only to painting, when he befriended Émile Zola, who would later become one of France's leading authors and social activists. They met when Zola moved from Paris with his parents to Provence, to Aix-en-Provence, where Cézanne's father was in the process of parlaying a prosperous hat business into a financial empire of sufficient consequence to provide his son an income that, however parsimoniously doled out, was sufficient to support his life of painting. The cities of Marseille and Aix brought Zola's father from Paris to build a dam in the mountains above Aix. There he got entangled in the local bureaucracies, including a fight with the little village at the bottom of the creek which foresaw, accurately, that the big cities were robbing it of its water. By the time Zola *père* got the dam underway, he was ten years older; he died from pneumonia contracted while working on the site and never saw it completed. Today his dam has been rendered obsolete by a much larger dam. But the dam brought Zola the son and writer and Cézanne the painter together. That, of course, was its principal function in advancing the cause of beauty.

They were passionate friends, in love with each other totally and completely in their late teens/early twenties—Walt Whitman's camerado love, the love of friends, the love of solitaries, the love about which I'm writing. Cézanne, the burlier of the pair, acted as Zola's defender in the rough-and-tumble of the schoolyard. "We have entered each other's body and soul," Zola wrote of his friendship with Cézanne. Six years later Zola decamped to Paris. After two weeks' silence, Cézanne begged for a letter from Zola, and later wrote him, "Ah! Yes, it would give me ineffable pleasure to see you . . . your mother told me that you would be coming to Aix . . . if I'd been a good jumper, I would have touched the ceiling, I leapt so high . . ." On hearing news of Cézanne's arrival in Paris, Zola wrote to Baptistin Baille, third of their Provençal trio of friends, "I've seen Paul!!! I've seen Paul, do you understand the full melody of those three words?"

Walt Whitman and Emily Dickinson, American solitaries with whom I will visit later, would have been entirely at home with the enthusiasm Cézanne and Zola shared. That such ecstatic friendship has fallen from our lives and art is due in part to our obsession with labels (gay, straight; married, single), and partly to our elevation of church-designed, government-sanctioned marriage as the apogee of human relationship. Somewhere, in part in service to capitalism, the notion took hold that to be worthy of celebration, love must be certified by government or church edict, when my experience has been that love does not submit itself to logic or reason, calendar or clock—that one may love differently, perhaps, but as intensely in a moment as across a lifetime. Ask any survivor of a war, or a plague.

It is that fact of selection—the intersection of chance and choice—that renders our friends dear, and the manner in which they literally personify the ever-changing currents of our lives. We must teach ourselves to value flux, but more than that, we must teach ourselves to value and attend to friends, not as way-stations between lovers or diversions from the real business of pairing up and marriage, but as relationships of first consequence in their own right.

Across from my parents' house rose a steep, forested hill—Pine Knob, and though it rose only six or seven hundred feet above the river bottoms of the Rolling Fork, I imbued it with significance. Like New England's Mount Monadnock for Thoreau and Emerson, like Mont Sainte-Victoire for Paul Cézanne, Pine Knob was emphatic in its declaration of solitude, a fixture of my literal and figurative landscapes—a manifestation of the "psychology of the earth," a phrase that originated with Cézanne's geologist friend Fortuné Marion.

I longed for Pine Knob to be more dramatic than it was. I wanted it to be a peak of the kind I'd seen in photographs, Mont Blanc or Mount Shasta, craggy and snow-covered and tall and above all majestic in its solitude, when in fact the charm of Pine Knob, I now realize, arose from the pleasing but entirely pastoral undulance it and the surrounding hills present to the eye. But for a child possessed of that volatile mix of ambition and imagination, a hillock may serve as Denali. The spirit works with what she has at hand.

And so in Aix, I took myself to the old man's mountain, to Mont Sainte-Victoire, to hike to the dam designed by Zola's father. My hike looped past an olive orchard and the ruins of a Roman aqueduct—that's the south of France for you, you're hiking in a wilderness and all of a sudden you come across an olive orchard and the ruins of a structure built two thousand years ago. Every once in a while, just often enough to lead one onward, the path gave spectacular views of the mountain, a living presence worthy of its lover's genius.

Mont Sainte-Victoire presides with calm assurance over the rolling plain of central Provence. With my first head-on view of its shimmering, weather-sculptured self, I understood that it was Cézanne's great and lifelong love, more than his wife and son, more even than his friends, and for good reason. To the north, the mountain descends in a long gentle slope, covered in oak and pine, with rosemary as the dominant undergrowth shrub—the scent alone was worth the minimal effort of the walk. To the south, the mountain descends sharply, a great white limestone mass, more than a thousand feet steep. Geologists tell us that 300 million years or so ago, the layers of a more ancient seabed were lifted and then, over time, folded forward, toppling over, or so I fantasize, under their own weight, in the way of some elaborate, layered French pastry. The lip of this great fold, thus exposed, eroded over time to make the mountain that I hike today. As a result of its orientation, the south face of the mountain is constantly in motion, as the near-constant Mediterranean sun passes across its face, so that shadow and light interplay over its gashes and crevices and canyons.

It must have been this particular feature—the mountain's capture and incarnation of light—that endeared it so to Cézanne; that, and its human scale (it reaches just over 3,000 feet, nearly the same height as Mount Monadnock), and maybe its manifestly feminine presence. The obvious visual evocation is of a breast, but rather than that I mean how in its splendid solitude it emanates warmth and embrace over the whole of its setting. Cubism waiting to be seen by an artist who could occupy beginner's mind thoroughly enough to see it and had the skill to execute what he saw, it is the embodiment of energy and mass, flux and permanence, life and death.

And then on cue, at the precise correct moment, an angel appeared on the trail, a young man with a head of dark curls who stepped out of a Botticelli painting, his cheeks flushed from exertion and his bare chest nicely displayed by the straps of his daypack. I smiled and mumbled, *"Bonjour,"* and he smiled and said, *"Bonjour,"* and I was left wondering if he was an apparition. School was in session that day, there was no reason a young man would be up on the mountain, and yet there he was. I turned to look back at him, but he continued down the long incline as I kept looking and looking, and then, at the very bottom, too far away for me to read any body language, he turned around and looked back at me, raised his hand in a half-wave, and continued around the bend.

> Like he on
> that last hill which lets him see his valley
> in wholeness, one last time, will turn and halt and pause,
> that way we live, forever taking leave.
>
> Rainer Maria Rilke, "Duino Elegy #8"

That *bonjour,* that magical apparition, that farewell wave, would not have contained its frisson, its certainty that somewhere, in some past or future or parallel and contiguous life, he and I were both seventeen years old in a world that would allow us to step into Cézanne's landscape hand in hand—none of that would have come to pass except that we, this young hiker and I, were each and both alone.

After several years Cézanne followed Zola to Paris, but he was too much a son of the country to be comfortable for long on city pavements. In 1869 he established what would become a lifelong relationship with Marie-Hortense Fiquet, with whom he had a son, Paul, to whom he was devoted. But neither he nor Hortense was well suited to domestic life, a fact exacerbated by Cézanne's concealing their stormy relationship from his father for seventeen years from fear that the elder would not approve the match and might terminate his allowance. Or such is the reason offered by his biographers; my sensitive bachelor's nose senses another solitary who understood that he was "not the marrying kind." After years in which they lived apart more often than together, the couple married in 1886, in part to assure Paul's paternity, though they had long since arrived at an agreement by which Hortense and their son lived in Paris and Cézanne lived elsewhere, devoting himself to painting, his true and lifelong lover.

Theirs is hardly the first marriage whose success required that the spouses live largely apart. Cézanne had an intense relationship with Hortense, but she was financially profligate, a burden in those years in which Cézanne was dependent on his father's beneficence, and she was as dismissive of her husband's painting as Zola had been supportive. Near the end of Cézanne's life she burned his mother's belongings and papers, an act that sent him howling into the woods in grief. For emotional support and sustenance he turned to friends, and, increasingly as he aged, to his painting—which is to say, to Mont Sainte-Victoire, the serene embodiment of his solitude. He painted Mont Sainte-Victoire over a hundred times, compared to some twenty-five paintings of Hortense—numbers in which I read, a little fancifully, the relative measure of his affection.

Critics and biographers have often presented Cézanne as breaking off his friendship with Zola after the publication of L'Oeuvre (The Masterpiece), Zola's portrait of a failed painter who commits suicide. But the recent major biography by the perceptive Alex Danchev minimizes this split in favor of the greater likelihood that, with age, Cézanne grew deeper into his particular character—solitary and contemplative—while Zola became an ever more public figure (though he, too, despite his marriage and many affairs, defined himself as a solitary). With his friendships, Cézanne was the platonic equivalent of the serial monogamist. By 1866 he had bonded with the Impressionist painter Camille Pissarro as his painting companion, correspondent, and source of emotional sustenance. Danchev is correct, I think, in perceiving Cézanne as not severing his friendship with Zola but as moving on—evolving. For many years he and Zola remained in touch but drifted ever farther apart, as Cézanne grew more conservative and Zola pursued his commitment to social justice.

Among the most remarkable of Cézanne's friendships was that with the pauper, poet, pianist, and philosopher Ernest Cabaner, whom he met—so the story goes—when Cabaner stopped him to ask to see the painting under his arm: *Bathers at Rest*, now housed in Philadelphia's Barnes Foundation collection. When Cabaner admired it, Cézanne gave it to him. It hung over the bed in the hovel of a room where already Cabaner was dying of tuberculosis. As evidence that Cézanne took the responsibilities of friendship seriously, in 1888, not long before Cabaner died, Cézanne organized a benefit for his expenses, with paintings donated by Dégas, Manet, Pissarro, and Cézanne himself, and a catalogue introduction by Zola.

In his late years, Cézanne was not entirely a hermit; he walked into town on Sunday afternoons to attend mass and dine with his wife and son before walking back to his studio, in the words of Rilke "a queer old lone wolf" who was in his last years "old and shabby and children followed him every day on his way to the studio, throwing stones at him as if he were a stray dog." All the same, Cézanne chose the discipline of long hours spent painting in solitude, lengthening those hours as he came closer to the great mystery, the great transition to that other form of life called death.

A facile explanation of those years would see in him an old man whose untreated diabetes (insulin would not be discovered for many years) drove him to the edge of madness, but artists and art are not in the business of facile explanations. Cézanne sought the sacred through his work, which he understood in religious terms; he accepted entirely the concept of a vocation to which he had been called. He writes of "being in front of the landscape and drawing religion from it."

Cézanne returned to Roman Catholicism in 1890, at the beginning of the intense final period of his life, and there is an emphatic connection between his return to the Roman church, his retreat into solitude, and his obsession with painting that geologic loner, Mont Sainte-Victoire. Working at the edge of diabetic collapse and with ravaged eyes, Cézanne paints, over and over, hallucinogenic visions of the "holy mountain of victory." Looking at these paintings, I'm given to consider how much modern art owes itself to religion and high blood sugar.

Cézanne was much taken with the medieval conception of character, which described four personality types corresponding to the body's four humors: short-tempered (choleric), optimistic (sanguine), easy-going (phlegmatic), and introspective (melancholic). For many years he named himself a choleric—the fiery blood of the south manifesting in the passionate painter—but as he aged he changed his self-characterization to melancholic. What distinguishes the melancholic, the French novelist Stendhal emphasized, is the search for solitude. Immersed in our society's fear and demonization of loneliness, the contemporary melancholic may spend years figuring out that she or he is temperamentally inclined to prefer living alone over the hypocrisies and accommodations and polite twaddle of society.

"Love is always a serious matter for the melancholic," Cézanne wrote. His statement struck me as explaining solitaries to ourselves as well as to any lover who might have the challenge and luck to stumble into relationship with us. How seductive and yet how dangerous, to love someone who brings such passion to one's life! Little wonder his marriage was so stormy.

Cézanne's fellow painter Jean Renoir described Cézanne at his easel: "an unforgettable sight . . . Cézanne . . . painting, looking at the countryside: he was truly alone in the world, ardent, focused, alert, respectful, sometimes coming away disappointed, returning without his canvas, which he'd leave on a rock or on the grass, at the mercy of the wind or the rain or the environment." Truly alone in the world, ardent, focused, alert, respectful: I know no better description of the virtues of solitude. Of these, "ardent" and "respectful" may be achieved in the company of another, but they take on different characters altogether when they manifest themselves in solitude, where of necessity the world, and not another individual, becomes the focus of one's ardent and respectful heart. But "focused" and "alert"? Remarkable indeed is the companion who will preserve silence long enough for these qualities to manifest themselves in tandem. "Only solitude, and the safety of solitude, permits of undertaking and achieving," wrote Cézanne's aesthetic mentor Delacroix.

Working in silence, I try to do each task, from stir-fry to writing, as silently as possible—no radio or television or speakerphone—a consummately pleasant exercise to see how quietly I can work, how completely I may cultivate a light hand. Everything is improved in the process, including the task, its doing, and its outcome.

The painter's task—the writer's task—the composer's task—the gardener's task—the cook's task—the teacher's task—the meditator's task—the solitary's task is to get out of the way, to dissolve and efface the self into the work at hand so as to permit its subject's essence to shine forth. Cézanne wrote, "You don't paint souls. You paint bodies; and when the bodies are well-painted, dammit, the soul—if they have one—the soul shines through all over the place."

In our age, which, like Cézanne's Belle Epoque, idolizes self-indulgence and self-expression, Cézanne teaches the power of restraint. From Cézanne, Rilke writes, we learn that "the very best—love—stays outside the work. Sentimentalists paint 'I love this here,' instead of painting 'here it is.' . . . [Cézanne] would certainly not have shown another human being his love . . . thanks to his strangeness and insularity, he turned to nature and knew how to swallow back his love for every apple and put it to rest in the painted apple forever." The paintings are the expression of what he sees, of the world in front of him, of his love of what is. Through his art the viewer becomes one with the painted object, whether with the apple or Mont Sainte-Victoire. His paintings can thus restore viewers to our true selves, without judgment or interpretation. In them the viewer becomes one with the universe, no duality, no separation between self and other, past and future and the eternal now.

Cézanne understood that every successful painting had to express the unity of all creation; it had to be so precise in its particularity, so thoroughly *seen*, that it became a stand-in for everything that is. "People think a sugar bowl has no physiognomy, no soul," he wrote. "But that changes every day, too. [As with people], you have to know how to take them, how to coax them, those fellows." I can say he's crazy—perceiving a soul in a sugar bowl?—or I can listen to what he's telling me, in his letters and in his work, which is that the sacred exists in every particle and atom, the sacred is what is, and my job is to pay sufficient attention so that I too can perceive the psychology of the earth—its living, feeling, expressive self, made manifest in rivers and seas and mountains and tornadoes and earthquakes.

In *Concerning the Spiritual in Art*, Wassily Kandinsky, a radical in his own right in his use of color, wrote that "Cézanne made a living thing out of a teacup, or rather in a teacup he realized the existence of something alive. He raised still life to such a point that it ceased to be inanimate. He painted these things as he painted human beings, because he was endowed with the gift of divining the inner life in everything. . . . A man, a tree, an apple, all were used by Cézanne in the creation of something that is called a 'picture,' and which is a piece of true inward and artistic harmony."

The artist or writer does not impose harmony on reality but—with sufficient reverence and diligence and selflessness and solitude—uncovers the harmony that is always there but that we conceal from ourselves out of a preference for material comfort and fear of the consequences a full and unreserved embrace of harmony requires. This faith in the underlying harmony roots itself in a love of and appreciation for nature, because nature, no matter how extreme the human abuse heaped on her, embodies a quiet, continual knitting and healing of life, ever dependent on death to make herself anew. "Art is a harmony parallel to nature," Cézanne wrote—not *identical with* but *parallel to* nature. Art of any kind, undertaken with attention and focus and as part of a commitment to discipline, is an effort at reenactment of the original creative gesture—the precipitation of the universe at the moment of its creation. That, I believe, is why we sing, paint, dance, sculpt, write; that is why any one of us sets out to create something from nothing, and why the creative impulse is essentially religious or, if you prefer, spiritual. We seek to recreate the original creative gesture, whatever or whoever set it in motion— the bringing into being of what is. We seek the center of beauty.

Once in his hermitage at Les Lauves, Cézanne had to install mesh on the windows, because the neighborhood children threw rocks at the home of the crazy solitary painter (van Gogh suffered a similar indignity, tortured by the children of Auvers-sur-Oise) who loved his solitude, who loved and respected himself enough to endure the trials of solitude, because only in solitude could he best give himself to his painting and through his painting to his God—and through his God to us. I know those rock-throwing children; I was once among them, on a winter evening when I was fifteen and riding around with the guys and somebody proposed that we throw rocks at the home of a man whose crime was that he lived alone in rural Kentucky. Of course there was some hidden, unvoiced homophobia, though at this time, deep in the country in the late 1960s, sex between men was barely known and spoken of only in epithets barely comprehended by their speaker. I write with great relief that I did not pick up a stone;

I did not walk up to the house and throw rocks but hung back at the car, feeling acutely my solitude in doing the right thing. But neither did I object, though I knew what we were doing was wrong.

It is a good question, whether witnessing evil in silence is as evil as the evil itself.

And I knew as well, even then—a vividly remembered gnawing in my groin—that I shared something with that man in the house, that I might someday be not outside but inside, like Cézanne in Les Lauves, listening to the rocks smack the walls.

No greater crime than solitude.

That is a story from my solitude, but it is not uniquely mine. On the contrary, in learning to live with the always present threat of violence, literal or implied, I have been given access to the place where so many people, women and small or feminine men, live all the time. All women or feminine men who have found themselves alone on a city street know this place. We have learned our lessons from the history of violence. At least once weekly I encounter that lesson acted out: I, a tall man, will be walking on a deserted city street when a woman turns the corner; seeing me, she crosses to the other side. I feel at the same time robbed of the companionable nod, the unjustness of her judgment, and the street-smart wisdom of her choice.

In 1898, Zola published his famous open letter "*J'accuse . . . !*," in which he set forth the case for anti-Semitism as the motivation behind the prosecution of Albert Dreyfus, a French army officer of Jewish descent who had been convicted of treason. Anti-Semitic painters, among them Renoir and Dégas, aligned themselves with conservative Roman Catholics against Dreyfus; those in his support were liberal thinkers and social justice activists, among them Pissarro, Monet, and Mary Cassatt, with Zola as their champion. Facing imprisonment and death threats, Zola fled to England. After a year he returned to Paris, where he died in 1902 under suspicious circumstances now widely considered to have been a politically motivated murder. The Dreyfus Affair divided France into bitterly antagonistic camps and may have marked the definitive end of Zola's friendship with Cézanne, who did not actively engage the controversy but who was by this time a devoutly practicing Catholic.

"I am only fit for isolation," Cézanne wrote, an observation born in part from the wild mood swings induced by his untreated diabetes. But throughout his life Cézanne had been known for his *inquiétude*, his restlessness or—a better translation—his anxiety. At a different moment he wrote to Émile Bernard, that gadfly among the great painters of France, "I can't bear for anyone to touch me; it goes back a long ways."

In his last years, Cézanne was treated shabbily by his brother-in-law, and in keeping with the loyalty that the marriage contract requires even in the presence of wrongdoing, his sister collaborated with her husband's perfidy. With the deaths of colleagues and friends (Zola, Pissarro, Cabaner, the dwarf painter Achille Empéraire), and the growing awareness of his own mortality, Cézanne grew ever more obsessed with his work—to his life project of remaking how we encounter the world. As Danchev writes, "For want of men there were trees," a sentiment I recommend to all solitaries. Cézanne painted trees, often. He built a wall around an olive tree outside his house so that it would not be damaged during construction, and in the evenings he embraced and spoke to it—like William Blake, another married solitary who talked to trees.

With Cézanne as his inspiration, Rilke writes, "All we have to do is to be, but simply, earnestly, the way the earth simply is." Rilke knows that for most of us, nothing could be more difficult. We live in our heads, we live for the future, we live for retirement. This is a challenge for those influenced by Western traditions—Jews and Christians and Muslims: all that living for a presumed messiah to come, or to return, or for a future day of judgment; all that longing for salvation when in fact paradise is right at hand ("the kingdom of heaven is at hand," Matthew 10:7), and our greatest troubles arise from not understanding that this is so. Paradise is in Cézanne's basket of fruit. Paradise is in the vase and pitcher on the table. Paradise, wrote the solitary and mystic Rumi, is a mirror in which you see yourself. In his paintings Cézanne hands us the mirror.

On my visit to Cézanne's studio in Les Lauves, I listened to the guide rattle on, a long story involving the olive trees that she claimed Cézanne preserved (Danchev writes that the original trees died in the great frost of 1956). I lost track of her French because I looked out the big north-facing window and a blizzard was blowing. Snow was swirling from the sky—big, fat, wet flakes of the kind that precipitate when the temperature is at freezing, covering all the pines and figs and olive and plane trees. I was enchanted; I lost my capacity to listen or speak French; I lost my capacity to speak at all in the swirl of cadmium white.

The guide withdrew to attend to some business, leaving me alone. I had the studio to myself and I was alone as Cézanne had painted alone, alone with the falling snow and the diffuse gray early winter light and the living presence of the old man, the painter, his easel and brush and palette and tea set and mugs and wall crucifix and human skull precisely where they were placed on the day of his death.

On my later, longer visit to Aix, on warm afternoons I walked past Les Lauves to the Terrain des Peintres, the flat ledge of land, now a small park, from which Cézanne often painted Mont Sainte-Victoire. Painters still work here, sometimes testing the colors of their palettes against the rock outcroppings or on the flagstone path, leaving a spoor of bright dabs of primary colors. The winter light, the flat northern light of Europe, so far north of Kentucky or San Francisco or Tucson, the light diffused in its long horizontal journey through moisture and dust, illuminates the mountain's flesh and bone, forest and stone. In this magical evening northern light, even human frailty and cruelty and suffering take their place in the solitude that draws us on, to the place where we are going.

Inscribed on a plaque at the park's edge:

Look at this Sainte Victoire! What élan, what imperious thirst for the light, and yet what melancholy, when evening restores its gravity. She breathes all blues from the air . . .

Paul Cézanne

CHAPTER 5

Formidably Alone

Walt Whitman and Emily Dickinson

TODAY I MADE LIME mousse, a recipe that starts with a custard of eggs, butter, and sugar—a promising beginning in my household. All recipes that involve binding—flour proteins to milk proteins, or thickening egg yolks—dislike the sharp edge of a metal spoon and favor the dull edge of wood, and so for the first time since filching my mother's butter paddle from the container that held her kitchen tools, I used it to stir the custard.

It's a small, short-handled, thick paddle, probably made of ash, the wood favored for hand-held cooking tools because it doesn't splinter and has no contaminating flavor. By the standards of Anglos in the American West, the paddle is unimaginably old. It was certainly used by my mother's mother, which would date it to the late nineteenth century, but likely it was harvested from a more ancient Appalachian forest. Probably it had never been out of Kentucky— although it may have come across the Appalachians from North Carolina in the late 1700s, that is possible, given its usefulness and the thrift and respect with which our ancestors regarded their tools.

It sits comfortably in the hand, and the path it makes as I stir the gradually thickening custard is satisfyingly blunt. It is as perfect a tool for the job as the ax to the tree, though being a woman's tool, it isn't so nearly enshrined in popular lore. It's too early to shift to present tense in this past-tense meditation but my stirring brings my mother effortlessly to mind, as she uses this same ash paddle to shape and pat strained butterfat into a mound of butter, finishing with her trademark three slashes across the top, using the paddle's blunt edge.

Emily Dickinson, an accomplished cook, scribbled poems on the backs of baking chocolate wrappers and recipes for coconut cake. The chocolate came from Paris, the coconut from a climate a lot warmer than western Massachusetts; each attests to tastes more sophisticated than those of rural Kentucky a century later, though my mother was a fine if self-taught cook in her own right. Her mother died (of kidney disease likely caused or exacerbated by too many pregnancies; she gave birth to eleven children) when my mother was not yet in her teens, meaning that my mother taught herself to cook, as many years later I would teach myself, though I had the considerable advantage of having watched my mother at work. With many children and, later, the community library to supervise, my mother developed an astonishing capacity to throw together the sort of sensitive concoction that causes me fits—caramel icing, say, or boiled custard, which the better-heeled and better-educated Dickinsons would have called *crème anglaise*—and then leave it on the stove, returning at the precisely correct moment to remove it from the heat. For those with limited cooking skills, these are recipes where the cook has perhaps thirty seconds, at most a minute, between success and an inedible mess. I ate my mother's cooking across a lifetime and memory counts on its ten fingers the number of times she burned the icing or curdled the custard.

Ash trees are disappearing now, as the American elms disappeared before them and the American chestnuts disappeared before
them, victims of the emerald ash-borer, an invasive insect that
arrived from Asia in the 1990s and that has few natural predators in
North America. Along with many of the woodsmen of Kentucky, my
brothers roam the forests, chopping down ash trees in keeping with
the generally held view that woodcutters should take them down now
while they still have life and usefulness rather than return two years
hence and find them rotting out. And yet how slow humans are to
learn to be humble before our power! Some biologists now believe
that had we left the elms and the chestnuts to fend for themselves,
some individual trees might have possessed or developed resistance
and would have survived to repopulate their landscapes.

As for that Dickinson poem scribbled on the back of the coconut cake recipe—Dickinson, like Thoreau, like my father, like me, a
seeker and finder of inspiration in the twice- and thrice-used object:

> The Things that never can come back, are several—
> Childhood—some forms of Hope—the Dead—
>
> > [#1515]

So much may today be added to Dickinson's poignant list of "things
that never can come back": for starters, American elms, American
chestnuts, and American ash trees, this last a species destruction on
a scale that will dwarf even our earlier losses of elms and chestnuts.

In the silence of my solitary walks I hear the voices of the trees.
I hear them singing of a solitude that admits no loneliness.

What poets—what human beings—seem at first glance to have less in common than Walt Whitman, the voluble, larger-than-life Good Gray Poet, and Emily Dickinson, the reclusive Belle of Amherst, Massachusetts? Whitman roamed the continent, venturing as far from his Long Island roots as New Orleans, as well as, in his imagination, to the grand open spaces of the American West. Dickinson rarely ventured outside her family home, and though in imagery and spirit her poems venture to the heavens, they are rooted in her garden and the nearby woods and pastures. In 1855, in the prime of his mid-thirties, Whitman self-published his great opus *Leaves of Grass*, then spent most of the rest of his literary life promoting, revising, and expanding it. Almost concurrently, Dickinson was writing almost 1,800 poems, few longer than twenty terse lines, few published in her lifetime. Whitman began his career as a journalist and was intimately involved with publishing all his life; Dickinson could write "Publication—is the Auction / Of the Mind of Man" (#788), a dismissal of publishing that borders on contempt. Whitman searched for beauty in big bold strokes, pronouncing on national identity and the destiny of empires. Dickinson writes from and of the intimate interior spaces: her parlor and garden and family orchard and, above all, her upstairs, southeast-facing bedroom.

It would be a stretch to draw an analogy between Whitman and Dickinson and my parents, who loved and threw a good party and who by example—our principal teacher—conveyed to their children that sex was a good thing in which one was expected to indulge. And yet my parents and my poets had a shared investment in the earthiness of life and an affection and respect for solitude. Had she not met my father, my mother told me gaily, she'd have run off to Brazil to be a flamenco dancer (her geography and cultural history were a little confused). As for my father, his mother thought her oldest son a good candidate to be a monk. "Well, I'd have *been* a monk," my father told me when I conveyed this observation to him, "except I cain't stand religion." In this I am my father's son.

Whitman and Dickinson and I share this powerful bond: we are "not the marrying kind." Whitman professed a desire to live with his lover Peter Doyle, an ex–Confederate soldier and Washington streetcar conductor almost twenty-five years his junior, but the two never cohabited. In 1873, after a debilitating stroke, Whitman moved in with his younger brother George, in Camden, New Jersey—but after an initial, amicable period, the men quarreled and, at the time of Whitman's death, were estranged. Like Dickinson, Whitman rejected a late-life marriage proposal—in his case, two proposals, each from a woman who wanted only to support him and bask in his glory. Like the Southern writer Eudora Welty, each poet seems to have evolved from longing for a partner to a calm acceptance of solitude as their destiny and their gift.

Whitman and Dickinson chose to write from and toward an idealized desire rather than inhabit the mundane reality of marriage. Each preferred the world of their vast and fertile imaginations over the confining world of fact.

I dwell in Possibility—
A fairer House than Prose—
More numerous of Windows—
Superior—for Doors—

[#466]

They are the poets of the American republic because in every word and punctuation mark they hold forth the beautiful ideal of democracy, of friendship, of camaraderie. They value the nation not as a collective power but for the safe haven it provides its individual citizens. Each did her or his best writing against the backdrop of the Civil War, the republic's most fraught and endangered years . . . until, perhaps, now, which is all the more reason to return to their work.

Neither bore children, though Whitman, in a statement that gives his biographers fits, claimed "five or six." How limited a vision that understands only conventionally conceived babies as their parents' children! *We* are their children, Dickinson's and Whitman's—we and the republic and any and all who have imbibed the American message of the primacy of the individual conscience. Between them, tilling fields cleared by their predecessor and mentor Ralph Waldo Emerson, Whitman and Dickinson taught us what it means to be American—how to build a nation of solitaries.

Both wrote under the inspiration of Emerson's Hindu- and Buddhist-influenced Transcendentalism. Through Emerson, both Whitman and Dickinson were exposed to the concept of a divinity that resided not in distant splendor amid gold-tinted clouds but in the fields and trees and in the recesses of one's heart.

> Some keep the Sabbath going to Church—
> I keep it, staying at Home—
> With a Bobolink for a Chorister—
> And an Orchard, for a Dome—

[#236]

I saw in Louisiana a live-oak growing,
All alone stood it and the moss hung down from the
    branches,
Without any companion it grew there uttering joyous leaves
    of dark green,
And its look, rude, unbending, lusty, made me think of
    myself,
But I wonder'd how it could utter joyous leaves standing
    alone there without its friend near, for I knew I could
    not . . .

                    "I Saw in Louisiana a Live-Oak Growing"

Wonderfully expressed, but: standing alone there without a friend near, Whitman *did* utter joyous leaves—leaves of grass, leaves still read today.

    There were perhaps proportionally more bachelors and certainly more spinsters in those days—more than half a million men dead in the Civil War made spinsterhood an enforced reality for many late-nineteenth-century women, though the phenomenon of solitude imposed by fate occurs following all major wars and among gay men of my generation following the 1980s, the terrible first decade of the AIDS epidemic. Even in my childhood, though, in the rural South of the 1950s, solitaries were a common phenomenon, with Miss Ermine the librarian and John the Baptist church organist and Ott and Duck Burks, bachelor brothers who lived off their wits in the forested hills, and Phil who ran the clothing store and Hannekamp the hermit, who had joined the monastery but found its rules too confining and retreated to a hut with a hand-pumped well at the edge of the abbey acreage; Jasper the last Cherokee and Ozetta who ironed our clothes and who, having raised uncounted children and grandchildren, lived alone; my great-uncles Nick and Herbert—all names that rise effort-lessly from memory, all solitaries.

Whitman and Dickinson were solitaries, and solitude was the vehicle of their imaginations. Each transcended gender duality—they are androgynes, shape-shifters in a way that may well be particular to solitaries. Each embodied and expressed both what it means to be a man and what it means to be a woman. Whitman, the man, writes in a loquacious, effusive, spiraling, "feminine" voice; Dickinson, the woman, writes with the muscularity and boldness and efficiency of a lumberjack. Virginia Woolf, a solitary within marriage, described the phenomenon among her British predecessors: ". . . a great mind is androgynous. It is when this fusion takes place that the mind is fully fertilized and uses all its faculties. Perhaps a mind that is purely masculine cannot create, any more than a mind that is purely fem-inine . . . the androgynous mind is resonant and porous . . . is natu-rally creative, incandescent and undivided . . ." Reading Whitman and Dickinson, feminine and masculine fall away and I inhabit what it means to be, not male, not female, but human—male *and* female, young *and* old, "undivided," i.e., unified in the self. The whole cata-logue of binaries by which society and convention define us falls away and I am tenderly brought to understand my solitude as a doorway to all that is, the "solitary turning" of the *uni* (solitary) *verse* (turning).

Critic and Whitman biographer Paul Zweig perceived the poets' affinity, writing, "Only Emily Dickinson was as formidably alone [as

Whitman]." Justin Kaplan, a more conventional, less perceptive Whitman biographer, drew from Whitman's lifelong bachelorhood the lesson that "perhaps [Whitman's] life had to be partial in order for his work to be whole." *Partial?* Walt Whitman, chronicler of nineteenth-century New York, nurse to Civil War soldiers in makeshift hospitals and under rains of bombs and bullets, voyageur down an untamed Mississippi, friend and associate of the greatest nineteenth-century minds, internationally famous—Walt Whitman, a *partial* life? The mind boggles. How *partial* must Kaplan's vision be—how blinkered our own vision, if we believe conventional partnership and marriage to be the only model of a complex emotional life. Is it not apparent that, like his Louisiana live-oak, Whitman's heart was whole unto itself?

Kaplan is hardly alone in thinking marriage or partnership as the heart's single-pointed goal. Adrienne Rich calls out fellow poet and critic Ted Hughes for making a similar assessment of Dickinson. Hughes describes Dickinson's creative outpouring of 1861–62 as owing itself to an "energy of desperation" arising from her grief over a "lost man" of an entirely presumed (by Hughes) "marriage that had been denied in the real world." Reading Rich's apt excoriation of Hughes's analysis, I am reminded of the misogyny and self-obsession of the male-dominated world of 1950s' and 1960s' literature, and the way in which, in a spectacular act of self-service, it viewed conventional marriage, where the woman served as her husband's amanuensis, as our emotional be-all and end-all.

Whitman's life was his book was his life, and he kept shuttling back and forth between them, issuing and reissuing *Leaves of Grass* in different editions and with sections lifted into books with different titles, but always writing and braiding the evolving story of a poet and a nation. Today's gay community claims him because of his "adhesiveness" to men—a term Whitman borrowed from phrenology, of which he was a fan, which translates into "friendship" or "camaraderie," as distinct from "amativeness," which makes the leap to physical contact. As he aged he got involved with ever younger men, writing them impassioned letters that are the more affecting, of course, because they never name their evident subtext—a subtext so evident that one begins to believe that, to express it so unselfconsciously, Whitman could not have been fully aware of it.

Of the soldier Lewy Brown, one of the hundreds that Whitman cared for in the Civil War hospitals in and around Washington, Whitman wrote: "Sponged him, fed him, cared for him, kissed him—a long kiss, a half a minute long." Whitman's prose offers many examples of this sort of writing, reinforced in turn by his poetry. Even today *Leaves of Grass* is bracing in its unabashed pansexuality, vibrating with an intensity that arises from the tension between the explicit subtext and the poet's inability (in earlier drafts) or refusal (in later drafts) to acknowledge it. In the "Calamus" poems, Whitman writes, "sullen and suffering hours—(I am ashamed—but it is useless—I am what I am;) . . . I wonder if other men ever have the like, out of the like feelings?"

Late in his life, when public discourse made its first tentative steps toward discussing the homoerotic subtext of his writing, Whitman denied it because, once it was pointed out, he was well aware that acknowledging it would reduce him from the greats to the footnotes. The English pioneer gay rights activist and "invert" John Addington Symonds wrote Whitman many letters, each more strongly worded than its predecessor, each suggesting that, in the "Calamus" poems—incorporated in their entirety in the third, 1860 edition of

Leaves of Grass—Whitman knew that he was taking up the subject of "inversion," i.e., homosexuality. In response after response Whitman dodged Symonds's implications until Symonds finally made a forthright attempt to pin him down, to which Whitman responded "that the 'Calamus' part has even allowed the possibility of such construction as mention'd is terrible . . . at the time entirely undreamed and unrec'd possibility of morbid influences—wh' are disavowed by me and seem damnable." Even in his private journals, when Whitman writes about Peter Doyle, one of his better-known loves, he erases "him" and writes "her": "avoid seeing her, or meeting her . . . or any meeting, whatever, from this hour forth, for *life*"—with the whole passage underlined once, and the last words underlined three times. And then twelve days later he meets Doyle again.

That Whitman might be only dimly aware of the implications of those lines may seem incredible to contemporary readers, surrounded as we are by explicit sexual imagery and physical passion and accustomed to clearly defined binaries ("gay," "straight," "male," "female"). Was his later rejection of their homoerotic subtext a retreat into the closet? Or are these contemporary labels imposed on a nineteenth-century man, who so idealized his loves and kisses that he thought of them as natural expressions of the love of comrades and not as sex? Even today we have only begun to acknowledge the measure in which, for the human imagination, if no words exist to name a phenomenon, it effectively doesn't exist. The word "homosexuality" was not coined until the 1880s, and did not come into common usage until after Whitman's death; possibly he never heard it. That Whitman could write impassioned letters to younger men without connecting that passion to the literal facts of sex is for me entirely plausible, since I belong to the last generation of people who experienced desire—all-consuming, adolescent, obsessive desire—without having a word to name what we were experiencing or receiving any indication that others shared our passion. Whitman would hardly be the first writer (or reader) to find epistolary love superior to its incarnated expression, but more to the point, in his days, the action to which his letters pointed—the real-life struggle of passion—had no precise correspondent in language, no words to name it aside from arcane formulations fumblingly borrowed from phrenology. That Whitman expressed his passion not explicitly but obliquely brought us *Leaves of Grass.*

I find it impossible to imagine either Dickinson or Whitman writing with a spouse or lifetime mate. Whitman was skittish around those women (there were several) who pursued him, but more than that, the letters and journals and prose and poetry make clear that unconsummated desire—or the ideal of friendship—provided the wellspring of his genius. Before the Civil War, he had entered a dry spell; it was ended not by his encounter with the violence of the war itself—he never saw a battle, though he tried—but in the caring for these wounded soldiers who passed into and eventually through his arms, onto their lives or deaths. Time and again the prose of *Specimen Days,* his fragmented journals of the war and the years following, rises to the standard of eloquence set by *Leaves of Grass.* Though he was an abolitionist and unabashed supporter of the Union, one of the more poignant aspects of *Specimen Days* is his equal affection for Confederate and Union soldiers. Desire, after all, is the ultimate democracy; the heart seeks its fulfillment indifferent or in forthright opposition to the law.

Paul Zweig, himself a solitary, wrote in *Walt Whitman: The Making of the Poet* of Whitman's ministering to the wounded and dying soldiers of the Civil War, that "In the wards . . . his homosexual ardor was not suspicious or shameful. It was medicine; it buoyed up the sick and the dying. There was no need to veil it in euphemism or . . . even to make poetry out of it." Later Zweig writes of the "fantasy" Whitman embroidered for the future: "He and [two of his hospital friends] would live together after the war and share everything and never be lonely again." Any young person (e.g., my father, e.g., me) might dream, as Whitman dreamed, of "solving" loneliness in a utopian community or, for the more conventionally inclined, in marriage. But, as Whitman came gradually to understand, the solitary's challenge is the conversion of loneliness into solitude. His life and writing bear witness to his slow coalescing of a unity of self—his movement away from the ideal of union with another and toward a full embrace of his solitude, through which he found union with everyone and everything.

Zweig considers Whitman's bent sexuality to be the source of his generosity, but (using my mother's walking stick to turn over the stone) I suggest the opposite—that homosexuality was one expression of his native generosity. It was his generosity that situated him outside Freud's "narcissism of the related" and placed him instead among those who today call themselves queers—outsiders to the received order, the status quo, the conventional household headed by a state- and church-sanctioned couple with 1.9 conventionally conceived children. Zweig characterizes Whitman as "lonely" because that's our received interpretation of solitude—anybody walking alone, reading alone, living alone, must be lonely, right? And to be sure, loneliness is an aspect of solitude—loneliness, popularly accompanied by the assumption that it is an aberrant condition that all healthy creatures avoid and is always accompanied by the diseases of madness, hoarding, and desperation.

But then I read this excerpt from Whitman's diaries, written not long before his death: "Every day, seclusion—every day at least two or three hours of freedom, bathing, no talk, no bonds, no dress, no books, no manners . . . Here I realize the meaning of that old fellow who said he was seldom less alone than when alone." I'm guessing, though this is only a guess, that the "old fellow" Whitman references is himself.

As for Dickinson, though she is always recalled as a spinster, late in life, like Whitman, she turned down a proposal of marriage—from a judge named Lord, to embellish the point. Though she bound her poems together in small sheaves, these were dismantled after her death, meaning that today readers can only speculate on their chronology or on Dickinson's preferred order of presentation, and thus how they might illustrate her evolution toward an embrace of solitude.

Dickinson repeatedly offers the observation that the solitary is given heightened appreciation of pleasures that others take for granted:

'Tis—Beggars—Banquets—can define—
'Tis Parching—vitalizes Wine—

[#313]

Those who have known hunger and thirst best appreciate food and wine; the outsider always has the most profound and comprehensive view.

Conventional religion has few married saints because outsider status is a prerequisite for what is commonly called sainthood. Not that all solitaries are saints—far from it. But the solitary may be given a particular vision of unity, of the sacred, of beauty. Because they belonged to no single partner, Whitman and Dickinson were open to and contained everyone (Whitman: "I am large, I contain multitudes"). Because they were not weighted down by the responsibilities of a particular relationship, they could uphold the ideal of relationship—which was for each of them not marriage but friendship and camaraderie: in Whitman's formulation, camaradoes.

By definition, marriage as it is conventionally practiced today excludes, defines an inside and outside, raises a battlement, digs a moat between its participants and others. That was never the case with my parents' marriage. My parents' door was always open, the big round table stocked with extra stools to accommodate last-minute guests and their friends who might appear as we were sitting down, the meal already on the table, and even so a stool would be pulled out, a table setting produced, a jar of homemade tomato juice added to stretch the soup, a plate served.

Whitman and Dickinson possess a consciousness too large to accept the inside/outside boundaries of conventional marriage. "I will not have a single person slighted or left away," Whitman writes. "In all people I see myself." Instead of marrying one, they married all, so that every one of us can claim both him and her as our spouse—a literary polygamy as vast as their readerships.

Relationship to a partner or spouse can be a thing of beauty—I have had and I have witnessed it—but I am more deeply touched by those who forge a relationship with all, who slight or leave away none. Perhaps that is what defines my solitaries—a reluctance to sacrifice openness to all for openness to one.

What are readers to make of Emily Dickinson, this dear, retiring soul, whose presumed-to-be-fragile heart carried the fiercest longings— for friendship, for beauty, for a response to the eternal, unanswerable questions, for a response to the notes and letters she posted daily to relatives and friends too busy or indifferent or preoccupied with their spouses and families and making and spending money to write back?

This is my letter to the World
That never wrote to Me—

[#834]

Compare Dickinson's poem to the opening line of a letter of Whitman's: "I do not know why you do not write to me. Do you wish to shake me off?" Or with her tart note to her brother Austin, who lived next door: "The next time you're not going to write I'd thank you to let me know."

How many of us possess the courage required to write—at barely thirty years old—

I like a look of Agony,
Because I know it's true—

[#241]

That blunt intolerance for social niceties is a hallmark of many of my solitaries. This woman, this spinster knew what it meant to field society's barrage of deceptions and connivings and manipulations without the shield and excuse of a spouse. Her life and work demonstrate the power available to the solitary who has achieved a single-pointed generosity—in Dickinson's case, giving herself, over and over, through her poems; in 1862, the year of carnage, Shiloh and Antietam, Perryville and Fredericksburg, she wrote over 350.

> I've nothing else—to bring, You know—
> So I keep bringing These—
>
> [#224]

She knew both loneliness and aloneness intimately, and from that knowledge summons the impertinence to give orders to God (the capitalized "You" of the previous citation?).

> God keep His Oath to Sparrows—
> Who of little Love—know how to Starve—
>
> [#690]

What is God's "Oath to Sparrows"? "[N]ot one of them shall fall on the ground without your Father [knowing]," [Matthew 10:29]. *I'm holding you to your promise to watch out for each of us sparrows,* Dickinson admonishes the great Gray-beard in the sky, *since we the smallest creatures know most acutely the importance of love.*

In response to the inquiry of her occasional editor and lifelong correspondent Thomas Wentworth Higginson as to whether she ever felt the need to be occupied, Dickinson wrote, "I never thought of conceiving that I could ever have the slightest approach to such a want in all future time . . . I feel that I have not expressed myself strongly enough." Her self-contentment brings my mother to mind, at ninety-plus years old obdurate in her preference for the risky solitude of her home over the safe companionship of a nursing home, she who sat for whole mornings and afternoons in her patio swing, naming the sparrows (starving of little love) that flocked to her feeder. "How can you name sparrows?" I asked her once. "One sparrow looks just like another." "No, they don't," she said. "Fred there, he looks shy but he'll peck at Pam's tail to get her to drop her food. Mike, he'll pick up a seed and give it to Pam." And I thought, *OK, whatever*, until on a spring day not long before her death I sat in that same porch swing, only this time I paid attention . . . and though Fred and Sharon were long gone, within fifteen minutes I saw how even here, amid these creatures so commonplace and at first glance indistinguishable, each was unique, each was a solitary.

As for my father, despite his days and weeks working in solitude, he was generous to a fault—perhaps seeking paternal affection of a sort that was, as best I can tell, never given him by his father, my grandfather, a binge alcoholic who died shortly before my birth. Whatever its roots, my father's generosity was sincere, as was his love of a good party. There was the Halloween party, where he borrowed a coffin from the local undertaker, made up my brother to look like a corpse, and had him lie in the coffin, to rise up at midnight. Or the Sadie Hawkins party, where the women dressed as farmers and invited the men to dance and for which he built a pen with two live pigs and a goat in one corner of the basement to achieve that authentic barnyard effect. That party ended sometime in the early morning hours, with my second oldest brother wrestling the squealing and deeply unhappy pig into the bedroom I shared with another brother. Solitary that I already was, I offered my sympathies to the pig.

But my fondest party memory dates from after my father's death, after the near-simultaneous deaths of my mother's oldest son and her second husband, after almost a decade of living alone, and still and always she was ready for a good party. New Year's Eve 1999, and my sister-in-law brought a board game modeled on Monopoly called Is The Pope Catholic? The rules allowed participants to persuade competitors to release them from jail by telling a story from their Catholic grade schools. Nobody went to jail all evening. Well into midlife, in the course of hearing my siblings' get-out-of-jail stories, I learned why my nuns and priests viewed me, the last of the family and on the whole an angelic child—a contemplative, after all; a solitary—with such suspicion. Having had my older siblings as students had prepared my teachers for the worst; unbeknownst to me, my siblings had a developed a reputation for rebelliousness learned, I now realize, less from my woodsman father than at the knee of my devoutly converted but thoroughly Protestant mother. The mystery is not that I never settled down with a life partner but why my siblings did.

Corresponding to the Community Chest element of Monopoly were cards with Catholic trivia questions; an incorrect response could lead to ejection from the game. One by one the teams missed responses and were eliminated, until there remained only my mother and me, and one brother and his Catholic-school alumnus friend. The final card challenged us to name the child who witnessed the appearance of the Virgin at Lourdes. I produced "Bernadette"— the competition insisted on a last name—my mother, the convert,

produced "Soubiroux." A pope is elected! In the succeeding pande-
monium, someone produced a fur-trimmed cardinal-red coat, a fur
cap, a staff, and rhinestone "2000" glasses. With much ceremony, we
crowned my mother the first woman pope.

You see, perhaps, why my family gave fits to the clergy of my
rural, deeply conservative Catholic town. You see, I hope, that "solitary" does not equate with "hermit"—I can easily see both Whitman and Dickinson, each heretical in their own ways, at that kitchen
table. You see, perhaps, that my impulse to solitude is at its root spiritual. Strong mothers make good solitaries.

Through their work—through their discipline—Dickinson and
Whitman came to understand solitude not as their enemy but as the
great lesson, their great teacher. Whitman in the hospitals, Dickinson
in her room: the self is the vehicle, the boat that takes us on the interior journey from loneliness to aloneness—that takes us on the journey from loneliness to solitude. "The cure for loneliness is solitude,"
writes Marianne Moore, an observation proven true so often in my
life that it has enabled me to understand the appeal of hermitry.

Whitman and Dickinson are mystics, a label for containing and dis-
missing those who perceive the true nature of reality. Their solitary
lives are one continuous act of selflessness, one long outpouring of
selfless love. All Dickinson's poems are love poems—poems from a
heart so infatuated with being alive, so responsive to the joy of the
universe, most particularly to that aspect of life called death, that it
trembles at the fantastic knowledge of itself and, like Whitman, can

barely withstand the onslaught of the senses. "Spring is a happiness so beautiful, so unique, so unexpected," Dickinson writes a friend, "that I don't know what to do with my heart. I dare not take it, I dare not leave it—what do you advise? Life is a spell so exquisite that everything conspires to break it." Whitman shocks us, even today, not as much by his explicitness, though he is that, but by his forthright embrace of self-love, his love of himself. I look at the shuck and jive of what passes for civilization, the oblivion of most people—I am including myself—to the beauty of what is, the fantastic, ongoing conversion of life into death into life, and I ask: Who is my better role model? The executive in his gated palace on a Florida beach? Or my poets, ecstatic in their solitudes?

And here, perhaps, lies the resolution of the seeming contradiction between the man who wrote "I celebrate myself" and the woman whose most famous lyric might be "I am nobody, who are you?": each poet goes through the self so as to transcend the self. "I" am simultaneously of greatest importance and of no importance. By becoming one with ourselves, we become one with the universe, with all that is.

The thing about living alone is that—exactly like living as a couple—after a long time it becomes either a habit or a practice. A habit is a way of living that you follow because it's what you did yesterday and the day before and the day before that. A practice is a way of living that you create and renew every day. A habit is a way of being that controls you. A practice is a way of being that you control—a deliberate (ad)venture into the unknown.

"A *Wounded* deer leaps highest"—a line that contains a life, a truth, a universe. Only in solitude could Whitman and Dickinson fulfill their destinies: become, in fact, not "partial" but whole—become fully realized, whole unto themselves, poets for the nation, poets for and of the people. Paradoxically, by becoming one with ourselves, the illusion of self and thus of separation falls away, and we become one with everyone, one with the universe, one with beauty.

CHAPTER 6

The Generosity of Bachelors

Henry James

MANY OF US LACK the patience or inclination for hours and days and years of what Henry James called the "mere twaddle of graciousness," and in any case a writer is called to design and cultivate a labyrinth of solitude, with the greatest writers' gardens featuring the most elaborated paths and beds.

Recalling his urban childhood in his memoir *A Small Boy and Others*, James writes:

> I see myself moreover as somehow always alone in these and like New York flâneries and contemplations, and feel how the sense of my being so—being at any rate master of my short steps . . . I watch the small boy dawdle and gape again, I smell the cold dusty paint and iron as the rails of the Eighteenth Street corner rub his contemplative nose, and, feeling him foredoomed, withhold from him no grain of my sympathy. He is a convenient little image or warning of all that was to be for him, and he might well have been happier than he was. For there was the very pattern and measure of all he was

to demand: just to be somewhere—almost anywhere would do—and somehow receive an impression or a vibration. He was to go without many things, ever so many—as all persons do in whom contemplation takes so much the place of action; but everywhere, in the years that came soon after, and in fact continued long, in the streets of great towns . . . wherever it might be, he was to enjoy more than anything the so far from showy practice of wondering and dawdling and gaping: he was really, I think, much to profit by it.

James is describing the life and spirit of the solitary contemplative—the person so sensitive to the world, so amazed by its spectacle, that she or he prefers sitting, watching, listening, and strolling over action. Of all creatures (think of a cat), possibly only humans would have it otherwise, so preoccupied are we with a vanished past or an illusory future.

In his sixties, James lived alone in Lamb House by the sea in Rye, England. Decades of writing made holding a pen an arthritic agony; his eyesight was failing. He hired a series of secretaries and dictated his last works. Though at first hostile to the noise of the typewriter, James soon came to depend on its clack and clatter as background noise to inspire his still fertile imagination.

This aged solitary summoned the strength to complete three long novels, at least one of which—*The Golden Bowl*—scholars count among the great creative achievements of English literature. I am daunted at the thought of the single-pointed focus, the con-centration, the presence to the here and now of the labor at hand, required to create, sustain, speak, and weave these threads into word tapestries as complex and evocative as the images created in cloth by the weavers of the Middle Ages. "The lonely celibate," he called himself in one letter, "who has to boil his own pot," and in a letter to his brother William, "your hopelessly celibate even though sexagenarian brother."

James may not have had much or any sex, and he never married, but he understood sex and marriage better than most of those who engage in both. Any of his later novels proves the point, but I offer as the smartest, most perceptive, most painful marriage proposal in English literature the encounter between the billionaire Adam Verver and the impoverished, charming, beautiful solitary Charlotte Stant in *The Golden Bowl* (1904), James's penultimate published novel and, in my judgment, his finest. If more people read *The Golden Bowl*, fewer marriages would fail—if only because fewer people would marry.

As a capitalist version of trial by ordeal, Verver, the widowed father of Charlotte's best friend Maggie, has Charlotte accompany him on a weekend jaunt as he bargains for ancient tiles from Damascus—"priceless" tiles, but a price will be named and paid. Along with the tiles, he exposes Charlotte "to the north light, the quite properly hard business-light, of the room in which they had been alone with the treasure and its master. She had listened to the name of the sum he was capable of looking in the face." By inviting Charlotte to observe him pricing the priceless, Verver undertakes an intimacy more risky than dropping his drawers: he has opened his checkbook. He has shown her a template for her future. She need only replace the priceless tiles with herself. So exposed is Verver now that the scene can lead to only one conclusion: "A man of decent feeling didn't thrust his money, a huge lump of it, in such a way, under a poor girl's nose . . . without seeing, logically, a responsibility attached."

Verver had broached the subject of that responsibility the evening before, as he and Charlotte sat by the sea. Charlotte offers as
ambiguous a response to his marriage proposal as ever spoken—"I
won't pretend I don't think it would be good for me to marry." She is
acutely aware that marriage will establish her in the awkward position of being her friend Maggie's stepmother as well as ending, or at
least restricting, her ongoing, secret love affair with Maggie's handsome Italian husband. But she is equally aware of the implications of
her fast-fading beauty and of Verver's proposal. "In fact, you know,
I want to be married," she says. "It's—well, it's the condition," and
such are the ways of the world that James has no need to spell out
what it's the condition for. Not great love, surely, and not great sex—
Charlotte already has those—but for access to power, entrance to the
club, financial security. Then as now, a man who possessed sufficient
wealth could lead a life indifferent to conventional morality. But for
women, as Charlotte well knows, marriage is "the condition."

Charlotte is torn between power and passion, between money
and sex, between her desire to be rich and pampered and her
secret, red-hot lovemaking with her best friend's husband—Verver's
son-in-law. (Oh, Mr. James, you are so wicked!) Over evening tea,
Charlotte—not at all our stereotype of a prim Victorian spinster—
tries to broker a deal in which Verver, ignorant of her illicit affair,
would support her not as his wife but as his kept mistress, a deal in
which, in fact, she obtains the best of both worlds while remaining
a solitary.

"Oh, you want to be taken care of. Very well then, I'll do it."

"I dare say it's very much that. Only I don't see why, for

what I speak of," Charlotte smiled—"for a mere escape from my state—I need do quite so much."

"So much as marry me?"

Her smile was as for true directness. "I might get what I want for less."

"You think it's so much for you to do?"

"Yes," she presently said, "I think it's a great deal."

Alas for love, Maggie comes to suspect the worm in the rose; she deciphers what's going on between Charlotte and her husband. For the first time, when her husband holds out the bait of his "infinite pressure"—sex—Maggie turns him down. In a turning point in their marriage, she decides to "keep her head," "achiev[ing] the feat of not losing sight of what she wanted," which is to separate Charlotte from her husband for good. Maggie asserts the power of money, *her* money, over her and her father's most priceless acquisitions—her spouse and her father's fiancée; she becomes, in fact, a businesswoman in the mold of her father. And in obedience to the awful, merciless, inexorable law of desire, once she stands up to her husband—once she says no to his "unfailing magic"—he feels for the first time a "hard yearning" for his wife. Between them, Verver and Maggie, father and daughter, divide the spoils and the Western world: the billionaire father marries Charlotte and removes her to Chicago; his wealthy daughter retains her husband in Europe.

James's magisterial biographer (five volumes) Leon Edel characterizes the conclusion of *The Golden Bowl* as "the only one [of James's novels] in which things come out right for the characters" because their marriages are preserved rather than destroyed. This is surely one of the greater miscues in American literary criticism, but Edel evidently believes that marriage is life's only satisfactory ending, even if it makes a commodity of beauty and entails the sacrifice of love on an altar of gold.

A decade earlier, James offered the scenario for his play *Guy Domville* to the managers of an English provincial repertory theater. In *Domville* James proposes a drama of a young man destined for a religious life who has to abandon his calling because he is the last of his line and thus under pressure to marry and produce a male heir. Domville (*Dom + ville*, i.e., "City of God," the title, as James well knew, of St. Augustine's fourth-century treatise establishing the foundations of the Christian church) has his choice of a young, beautiful, wealthy woman or a similarly endowed widow, even as in his heart he believes that to marry would be in service to worldly selfishness—to bind himself to a life of material ease and endless afternoon cricket and teas. Domville quietly arranges for each woman to marry the man she really loves, sacrificing the worldly comforts of marriage for the more austere and demanding vocation to the common good embodied in solitude and celibacy. Like James, he chooses the priesthood, though James sacrificed himself on the altar not of the church but of art.

James fought hard to find a producer for the play. The first whom he approached asked him to devise a happy ending—one in which Domville marries. James larded his response with acid italics: "To make a Catholic priest, or a youth who is next door to me, *marry,*

really, when it comes to the point, *at all*, is to do the spectators a dis-
agreeable and uncomfortable thing."

James finally located a producer willing to take on the project,
though only after cuts that in James's view "abbreviated and simpli-
fied [the play] out of all close resemblance to my intention." Much
of literary London attended opening night—George Bernard Shaw
and H. G. Wells were on hand to write reviews. When at the end of
the play the manager brought James to the stage for a bow, the balcony erupted in jeers and catcalls. Edel reports evidence that these
critics were planted by James's literary enemies, but, having read the
script, I can report that, at least as published, it is—well, not very
good. It's a play written by a novelist, not a playwright.

Domville closed after its contracted thirty-day run. The gods
never missing a chance to mock mortals, it was followed in the same
theater by Oscar Wilde's sparkling, wildly successful *The Importance
of Being Earnest*, a tale of the conniving, manipulation, and selfishness required to arrange and sustain a marriage. Four months after
its opening, Wilde was arrested, tried, convicted, and sentenced to
two years at hard labor for "crimes of gross indecency." The police
immediately closed the play. Constance, his long-suffering wife,
resumed her maiden name and removed herself and their children
to Switzerland. Wilde never saw them again, and one of the most
painful passages of *De Profundis*, his letter from prison, laments
their loss.

But I am concerned here with the message of *Guy Domville*
rather than its fate. In his letters James makes clear that the play's
subject is "magnanimity" (for which term one can seamlessly substitute "altruism") and that Domville's decision illustrates his rejection

of worldly selfishness, as epitomized by marriage, in favor of "his old ideal"—he "renounces his personal worldly chance, sacrifices himself and makes the others happy." This understanding of a happy ending founded on a solitary sacrifice—the Christian message summarized in a phrase—was too complex for the English theatrical audience, or maybe any theatrical audience. How could an audience embrace the choice of altruism over selfishness? How could they accept that a life of celibacy and solitude was morally equivalent, perhaps superior, to the security, comfort, and companionship of fortress marriage? How could they accept that solitude, not marriage, is the more selfless choice?

What James's nineteenth-century audience wanted—what twenty-first-century audiences want—is validation, not complication, of our life decisions. Without the avalanche of messages telling us that marriage is our most noble means of self-sacrifice, we might choose to sacrifice ourselves in other ways—we might sacrifice ourselves not for our individual wealth but for the common wealth. James was dramatizing a radical gloss on our definitions of generosity and self-sacrifice. For James, though solitude and celibacy were trials, they were also the most generous paths—and as such, in their ways, the most magnanimous, if not the most conventional, of endings.

In a letter congratulating his brother William on his marriage, James wrote, "I believe almost as much in matrimony for other people as I believe in it little for myself." In another letter he wrote, "I am too good a bachelor to spoil. That sounds conceited—but one may be conceited in self-defense." The verb that strikes me in that sentence is "spoil." Taken into consideration along with "almost" ("I believe almost as much in matrimony for other people") as well as "self-defense," I find in the famously reticent James a clue to his opinion of the institution of which he is one of our most astute observers. "I shall never marry," he wrote to his longtime friend and correspondent Grace Norton. "I regard that now as an established fact. Singleness consorts much better with my whole view of existence (of my own *and that of the human race* [italics mine]), my habits, my occupations, prospects, tastes, means, and situation 'in Europe,' and absence of a desire to have children, fond as I am of the infant race."

This is not to characterize his solitude as a matter of pleasant days spent in blissful contemplation. As he aged he became fearfully lonely. Shortly after the Wilde trial and conviction he decamped from his beloved London for rural Rye, a relocation suggesting, after Wilde's trial, that he may have had encounters of his own that would justify fleeing the dramatically altered social environment of London, where now the testimony of housekeepers and rent boys could send a man from the upper classes to prison.

In his sixties James became infatuated with two young men, each of whom returned his affection but neither of whom was likely his lover. Both left him to continue their lives elsewhere. For "the lonely celibate" to encounter such departures late in life must have been heartbreaking indeed; the heart, like the rest of the body, grows more fragile with age. Though at Rye James entertained leading literary lights of the day—Stephen Crane, Joseph Conrad, Ford Madox Ford, Edith Wharton—he writes, "The days depart and pass laden somehow like professional camels—across the desert of one's solitude." He counsels an aspiring correspondent, "[Writing] is solitude.

If it runs after you and catches you, well and good. But for heaven's sake don't run after it. It is absolute solitude."

In the end technology offered James some consolation: the sound of the typewriter—his particular typewriter—without which later in his life he could not work; and, while his strength endured, his bicycle—providing both the head-clearing relief of exercise and the comforting spectacle of the world moving past slowly enough to observe but fast enough to leave interior demons in the dust, at least for the duration of the ride.

I asked a literate friend and fan of James whether, given that late in life Henry James fell in love with a sculptor, employed a bachelor typist, and hired a boy as gardener who later becomes his valet, it is possible to imagine that he was having sex. "No," my friend answered firmly. "I agree," I said, "but what leads us to say this with such confidence?" My friend thought for a moment. "Because of the arabesques and convolutions of his mind as revealed through his writing."

Somewhere around 1900, for the first time, so far as I am able to determine, since his youth, James shaved his beard. He looks younger without it, but I see him as revealing himself, late in life, to the world. Heavy beards are masks, concealing their wearers' involuntary, revelatory twitches and grimaces, and no one was more adept at or interested in concealment than James. Removed from London to the simple life of the countryside, allowing himself to perceive, perhaps for the first time, the implications of his attraction to men, James makes a small and belated gesture of lowering his guard, removing his mask.

Not that he jumps into bed or makes a move to requite those passions, but the late novels are driven by longing, and while this has been a lifelong subject for James, in no place is the energy more concentrated. "Concentrated?" one might object, in speaking of those monumentally diffuse novels, but I hold my ground: they are convoluted and they are certainly long but their very length demands an intensity of focus almost impossible for ordinary mortals to conceive—and this from a man in his sixties.

Ostensibly James took to dictating his novels because of arthritis, but I can testify that, living alone, one perfects the art of talking aloud to oneself. Dictating his work brought James the company not of a single speaking voice, but of the many speaking voices that populated his fictional world. I have a vision of James dictating to his typists—the "silent Scot" William MacAlpine, and more notably Mary Weld, MacAlpine's crocheting successor—and in the process making love with and to each of those long sentences. For as all lovers worth the effort and all vocalists know, the mouth and the tongue are the most erotic human instruments.

A certain kind of wisdom is given only to the outsider, the court jester who looks on as others go about their business. Edel understands that early in his life James, his subject, "substituted close observation of life for active participation." But Edel's use of "substitute" presumes an either/or choice between observing life and living it, when all my solitary writers and artists and composers demonstrate the opposite, i.e., that honing the powers of observation enriches the whole of one's life, that an equally rich life is to be found in contemplation as in action. How many of those Edel would call "active participants" in life have led lives as rich and varied as that of Henry James or Eudora Welty? Edel seems incapable of conceiving that a rich emotional life might happen outside the norms of marriage, children, cats in the yard, dog in the manger. And yet all my solitaries (Whitman, Thoreau, Dickinson, James, Moore, Welty, Hurston . . .) suggest that as full or fuller a life arises in and from a disciplined solitude. James, who panned Whitman in an early review, gave the last years of his life to emulating him, nursing soldiers from the battlefields of World War I as Whitman had nursed soldiers of the Civil War.

Like Whitman and Dickinson, James turned down a marriage proposal from a wealthy suitor who asked only the pleasure of his company in exchange for her financial support. Each writer preferred solitude to companionship under the yoke of society. "Things for Henry James glow, flush, glimmer, vibrate, shine, hum, bristle, reverberate," wrote poet and fellow solitary Marianne Moore. "Joy, bliss, ecstasies, intoxication, and a sense of trembling in every limb . . . Idealism . . . willing to make sacrifices for its self-preservation was always an element in [his] conjuring wand." Note Moore's invocation of "sacrifice," which Thomas Merton named as the most essential quality of true love.

Idealism willing to make sacrifices for its self-preservation. So this is the heart's yin/yang, strophe/antistrophe, matter/energy, to be counted among the great inextricably intertwined opposites: greater suffering born of openness and sensitivity, greater wisdom born of openness and sensitivity.

CHAPTER 7

All Serious Daring Begins Within

Eudora Welty

. . . writing is a solitary job—that is, nobody can help you with it, but there is nothing lonely about it. I have always been too busy, too immersed in what I was doing, either mad at it or laughing at it to have time to wonder whether I was lonely or not lonely; it's simply solitary. I think there is a difference between loneliness and solitude.

Eudora Welty,
University of Virginia lecture, 1958

MY ONLY MEETING WITH Miss Welty (my childhood manners assert themselves; thinking of her regal self by given or family name alone is a challenge) opened with a disagreement. "So wonderful," Miss Welty said on visiting Stanford in the mid-1980s, where I was a Stegner Fellow, "to encounter another Southerner way out in California." "I beg your pardon," I said, "but I'm not from the South. I'm from Kentucky." "Well, *we* thought of Kentucky as the South," she responded, and told how, on returning from visiting relatives in Ohio, her grandmother made her father stop the car the moment they crossed the Ohio River at Cincinnati so she could step out and set her feet on Southern soil. Now, many years later, I concede her point. Kentucky is the quintessential border state and any careful reader of its many writers will find its bipolar character embodied in their work, but it is surely more South than North, however fierce its insistence on its unique, rich, problematic blend.

On the final day of that Stanford visit she spoke to an undergraduate seminar. After her remarks, a student raised her hand. "Miss Welty," she asked, "how is it that you, who have never been married, can write so eloquently of love?" We held our collective breath—I could feel her hosts quail at so intimate an inquiry in such a public setting. After a moment Miss Welty said, simply and powerfully, "I have known love. I have been lucky, in love." And that was the end of that.

However rooted in naiveté, the student's beginner's-mind question was apropos. How is it that so many of our most perceptive writers about romantic love and marriage never experienced these in conventional ways? Jane Austen, Henry James, Eudora Welty—our resident experts on human relationship, none wed, all solitaries.

Named in the 1980s by the eminent critic Guy Davenport as "America's greatest living writer," Eudora Welty was born in Jackson, Mississippi, in 1909, the second child—an older brother died in infancy—of prosperous parents who would have two more sons. Her father died when she was a child. Her brothers both "preceded her in death," as the local obits say, the second dying in 1966, four days after their mother, leaving Welty as the sole survivor of her immediate family.

Between 1936 and 1955, she published almost all the stories for which she is justly remembered. Then came a period of relative quiescence before the appearance, in the early 1970s, of two novels, the longer of which (*Losing Battles*) was fifteen years in the making. She gathered her critical essays into an instructive anthology, *Eye of the Story*, and published her *Collected Stories*, as well as the short, marvelous memoir *One Writer's Beginnings*.

In her youth, Welty ventured into the great world, living in the upper Midwest, New York, and briefly San Francisco, but in her late twenties she returned to Jackson and lived there for the remainder of her life. Her reasons for remaining in Mississippi were as complex as those that govern any writer's life, but finances and family must have played a significant role. Had she lived in New York, she would have been bound to the wheel of making money. In Jackson she could live with and care for her ailing brother and aged mother while leading the life of an artist, writing but also painting, gardening, and taking photographs, the last a serious vocation that led to exhibitions and publication. At a relatively young age she grasped that she needed an anchor to keep her grounded; her anchor would be the house and family and the place where she grew up.

A Hollywood-driven perspective might imagine that conventional love and marriage evaded her because she was plain. Suzanne Marrs, Welty's biographer, reports that Katherine Anne Porter said to Welty, "You will never know what it means to be a beautiful woman." The comment reveals more about Porter's conception of beauty than Welty's appearance, though one hopes it earned Porter a few centuries in some lower level of Purgatory.

And yet plenty of plain people partner and/or marry. What's going on here is something more profound than mere mien. Even in early photographs, Welty is radiant with her unabashed horse-toothed smile—somehow she found in her youth the self-possession to embrace it as her signature feature. In meeting her I felt over-whelmingly that, when she looked in the mirror in the morning, she liked what she saw, because what she saw she had consciously cre-ated. She was her own spouse.

The men who knew her best considered her spinsterhood a calamity. Novelist, memoirist, and friend Reynolds Price claimed that after her first story, "Death of a Traveling Salesman," she never wrote about "the potentially killing weight of sheer loneliness," and that "the lifelong absence of an intimate love silenced her before she was ready for silence. . . . it left her somehow deeply puzzled for the last decades of her life"—an interesting observation coming from Price, himself a solitary who lived alone "by choice." Biographer Marrs reports that William Maxwell, for many years Welty's fiction editor at *The New Yorker*, "felt that Eudora needed someone to share her life and her home and her sorrows." And yet how strange to think of the accomplished, profoundly wise, fully realized Miss Welty in terms of absence and need!

In *One Writer's Beginnings*, Welty identifies her great subject as "human relationships," but I would refine that description to "human aloneness," whether apart from others or in relationship. Possessed of the outsider's capacity to see through and beyond the Hollywood fantasy of romantic love, she understood early that marriage does not end and in fact often exacerbates loneliness, and that we are all of us, married or single, finally solitaries. For what is coupling—even dear coupling, even happy coupling, even sacred coupling—but an unwinnable shell game played with the gods?

She evolved from a believer in "true love—something of gos-samer and roses" (the phrase is from her early romantic fable *The Robber Bridegroom*) to a more sober understanding of relationships and her place as their chronicler. To a friend she writes, "I am a facer of facts by now, I think, though it took me a long time—took being a writer, perhaps, and of course it took being a reader." While still in her forties she writes of a newspaper interview that it "made her out a complete fool, professional Southerner and old maid and I'm just one of those," and it is characteristic of her dry wit and unsparing self-knowledge that she leaves to her reader to decide which label she claims.

Not that Welty paints spinsterhood as an unqualified liberation. In her story "June Recital," the teacher Miss Eckhart offers music lessons in a small Southern town in the years following World War I, where her German, immigrant roots reinforce her status as an outsider. Welty writes of Miss Eckhart, "Her love never did anybody any good," a kid-glove brutal assessment of the spinster's life worthy of Austen, especially when one considers that, of all Welty's characters, she claimed the greatest empathy with Miss Eckhart. In her memoir Welty writes,

I did bring forth a character with whom I came to feel oddly in touch. This is Miss Eckhart, who is formidable and eccentric in the eyes of everyone [and] is scarcely accepted by the town . . . Miss Eckhart came from me. There wasn't any resemblance in her outward identity . . . what counts is only what lies at the solitary core . . . what I have put into her is my passion for my own life work, my own art. Exposing yourself to risk is a truth Miss Eckhart and I had in common. What animates me and possesses me is what drives Miss Eckhart, the love of her art and the love of giving it, the desire to give it until there is no more left.

At the story's end Miss Eckhart tries to burn down the house where for years she has rented a room. The penultimate paragraph, a real chiller, reads, "Both Miss Eckhart and Virgie Rainey ["Virgin" Rainey, her only talented student] were human beings terribly at large, roaming on the face of the earth. And there were others of them—human beings, roaming, like lost beasts."

In "Powerhouse," a fictionalized portrait inspired by seeing Fats Waller play a Mississippi roadhouse, Welty writes, "Of course, you know how it is with them—Negroes—band leaders—they would play the same way, giving all they've got, for an audience of one. . . . When somebody, no matter who, gives everything, it makes people feel ashamed for him." Juxtaposing Welty's observations, from *One Writer's Beginnings*—"What animates me and possesses me is . . . the love of . . . art and the love of giving it, the desire to give it until there is no more left"—and from "Powerhouse"—"When somebody, no matter who, gives everything, it makes people feel ashamed for him"—I understand that, watching Fats Waller give his all for an audience of white folks, Welty saw him acting out a different version of her own destiny, in which she gave everything not to one person but to all her readers, harnessing her boundless love into art. It is that generosity—the generosity of solitaries—that as much as her flawless prose and perceptive eye draws me to her work.

As for "people feel[ing] ashamed for him"—"ashamed" is an unsettling choice of words. Ordinary mortals, servants to desire and convention, must feel shame in the presence of such selfless generosity, such generous giving away of the self. Otherwise we might have to turn and look, really look inside ourselves and question our cultural assumption that the best way to give of ourselves lies through conventional marriage and conventional families, in which law and society and genetics are always at hand to define and enforce limits on our generosity.

I return to the hamlet where I grew up and I face many times the question I received at a high school friend's funeral: *Are you married? No? Ever been? No? Children? No?* And in the triple negative I understand my place in this subculture, which is precisely and exactly no place. "No Place for You, My Love," Welty entitles one of her best stories, and, though she very much made the best of her situation, life as a spinster in the Deep South could not have been an easy path.

So many of Welty's tales—"Death of a Traveling Salesman," "A Worn Path," "No Place for You, My Love," "Bride of the Innisfallen" come immediately to mind—are road stories. Welty understood that every life, every story—its writing and its reading—is a journey, a narrative that takes place both inside and outside time. We sit down to the story and when we finish it the clock tells us that an hour has passed, and yet for the duration of that hour we have been outside of time; we have transcended time, we have conquered time in one of the few entirely adequate ways given to us. Only the marathon runner, high on endorphins, or the heroin addict, or the besotted lover in the presence of the beloved, or the meditating hermit, or the traveler suspended between departure and destination may understand as fully as the dedicated reader what it means to live outside time—to live, in fact, not in the past or the future but in the mystic's eternal now.

And how Welty loved to travel!, undertaking all but one of her several trips to Europe alone, at a time when a woman traveling alone was an invitation to suspicion and pity. For to travel alone, as every solo traveler knows, is to be a moving target. Suspended between hither and yon, we step outside time—another way of cheating death. Rather than perceiving her travel, as Reynolds Price described it, as "an anesthetic for loss and grief," is it not closer to the mark to see it as the very fulfillment of love, postponed throughout those years she cared for her infirm relatives? For travel is a stimulus to the imagination, and imagination is the very path to love.

The solitary traveler is a repeating device throughout Welty's fiction. In "Death of a Traveling Salesman," the protagonist moves alone across the landscape to his encounter with death. In "A Worn Path," the elderly black grandmother moves alone across the landscape to seek help for her ailing grandchild. In "No Place for You, My Love," the solitary strangers, each unhappily married, meet by chance in New Orleans and journey, alone together, across the great, mystical river into the land of forgetfulness. There they hazard a kiss, only to draw back into their solitudes. In "Bride of the Innisfallen," the wife, on the lam from her husband, travels alone across the darkened English countryside, suspended between one place and another, until she emerges alone into the bright dawn of Ireland.

Almost all Welty's women are stubborn solitaries. Those who marry are usually unhappy for having done so—see the nameless protagonists of "No Place for You, My Love" or "Bride of the Innisfallen." The first-person narrator of "Why I Live at the P.O." is famously unreliable—she's vain and garrulous, a walking compendium of spinster stereotypes. All the same, she decamps from her family's house to set herself up in solitary splendor at the post office, and she is mighty proud of herself for doing so. In "The Wide Net," the young wife, three months pregnant, disappears, leaving her husband a letter in which she writes that "she would not put up with him . . . and was going to the river to drown herself." And what of Miss (*not* Mrs.) Snowdie MacLain in *The Golden Apples*, who marries King MacLain but stays with him exactly long enough for him to impregnate her in a golden shower invoking the visit of Zeus to Danaë? Miss Snowdie got from the King what she wanted—an evening's pleasure and his demigod's genes. After that, she was well shut of him, free to raise their child alone. In this she was a pioneer: contemporary demographics bear out that, given an opportunity to manage conception and to support themselves and their children, more and more women are choosing Miss Snowdie's path, leaving the showerer of gold to his promiscuous ways and striking out on their own.

I'm brought to wonder whether William Maxwell and Reynolds Price rooted their observations about Welty's loneliness in their male incapacity (or unwillingness) to comprehend a woman who so clearly *enjoyed* men and occasionally *loved* men but so evidently didn't *need* men. How likely was such an extraordinary and fully realized woman to find a mate worthy of her love? And if she found that person, how would they have fashioned a life in Jackson? Welty had the wisdom to embrace her limits early on and then to use them as the foundation for a glittering solitary life, a choice deserving of admiration and emulation, for those courageous enough to define and follow their particular versions of her journey.

Perhaps some truth resides in Price's contention that after "Death of a Traveling Salesman" (her first published story) Welty never again wrote about "the killing weight of sheer loneliness." If so, that was because she was writing away from loneliness and toward an embrace of aloneness. I trace an evolution from the fear of loneliness that informs "Death of a Traveling Salesman" to her later, more sophisticated embrace of aloneness—i.e., deliberately chosen solitude. In "Traveling Salesman," the protagonist makes an eloquent plea for a companion:

> I have been sick and I found out then, only then, how lonely
> I am. Is it too late? My heart puts up a struggle inside me,
> and you may have heard it, protesting against emptiness . . .
> It should be full, he would rush on to tell her, thinking of his
> heart now as a deep lake, it should be holding love like other
> hearts. It should be flooded with love. . . . Come and stand
> in my heart, whoever you are, and a whole river would cover
> your feet and rise higher and take your knees in whirlpools,
> and draw you down to itself, your whole body, your heart too.

The salesman's plea to the universe is the poignant appeal of a twenty-seven-year-old idealist, unmarried, living with aging relatives in her childhood home and fearful of spinsterhood.

But compare that passage to this, from "Bride of the Innisfallen," published almost twenty years later: A woman, never named—in her anonymity she may stand in for any young wife—is aboard a train taking her across England to the coast and thence by ferry to Ireland. She "is leaving London without her husband's permission." "'Let him wish her back,'" she thinks as she opens the window of her train compartment to lean out "into the wounded night." "Love with the joy being drawn out of it like anything else that aches—that was loneliness; not this," Welty writes, with "this" being the exhilaration of traveling alone, the exhilaration of experiencing love *without* the joy being drawn out of it. "I was nearly destroyed, she thought, and again was threatened with a light head, a rush of laughter . . ." The anonymous wife's solitary flight represents a leap, not into loneliness but into aloneness: liberation in solitude.

On the story's last page, the wife contemplates sending her husband a telegram letting him know that she's safe. She scribbles on a scrap of paper: "'Don't expect me back yet' was all she need say . . ." But then she recalls their parting quarrel—"What was always her trouble? 'You hope for too much,' he said." At the recollection, she drops her draft telegram into the gutter. "The girl let her message go into the stream of the street, and opening the door walked without protection into the lovely room full of strangers." Contrast this ending, revised for the 1982 edition of Welty's collected stories, with her original ending, published in *The New Yorker* in 1951: ". . . [the girl] let the letter slide, skim into the wet stream of the streets, and turned into the bar." The comparison is telling: between 1951 and 1982, the runaway wife loses her "protection" and gains in its stead a "lovely room full of strangers."

In these stories Welty is writing of independent women—solitaries—who have always existed but whom society has treated with dismissal and disdain because of . . . what? Fear of their power? Envy that they have escaped men's power? Solitude in the "lovely room full of strangers" is preferable to the "protection" of marriage. Better to live alone in "pure joy" than to compromise that joy with someone unable or unwilling to summon the courage required to live in its bright light. Better to inhabit one's hopes, joys, and disappointments fully, if alone, than to conform them to the sensibility of someone less realized. And who could be as realized as Miss Welty, who had come to her fullness through the struggle and discipline of her art?

In a letter Welty wrote, "When a story is going on, then you feel things highly and even more than you knew you might, and they reveal themselves to you in a way that gives some pain too, but in the work something is resolved, and let go." Welty's particular pain was to live as a solitary in a resolutely coupled world. Her stories were the construction of a narrative and artistic use for that pain, her means of making peace with her destiny. Having worked out that peace in three collections of stories, she moved on to different challenges.

Published in 1970, *Losing Battles* is an epic novel about a domestic topic—the reunion of an extended family in Mississippi hill country. Two years later, with *The Optimist's Daughter*, Welty returns to portraying a solitary woman, though the focus here is less on her interior life than on how and whether any conventional community can accommodate the solitary. Laurel, who went north and stayed there, has returned to her childhood home for the funeral of her father, "the Judge." Mrs. Chisom, matriarch of the double-wides, clucks over Laurel because she hasn't "father, mother, brother, sister, chick nor child. Not a soul to call on, that's you." The mayor, part of the educated, prosperous classes and a lifelong friend of the Judge, cries, "What do you mean! This girl here's surrounded by her oldest friends!" To which Mrs. Chisom sniffs, "Friends are here today and gone tomorrow. Not like your kin."

Mrs. Chisom represents the old guard—the conventional way of doing things, in which marriage, because it arose from and centers around the transfer of property and the continuation of the inviolable chain of blood kin, must be the cornerstone of any enduring relationship or society. Compare that perspective to the words of Jesus, who famously tells his followers to "let the dead bury the dead." Both the Buddha and Jesus left behind their conventional families to establish instead a chosen family of solitaries; as the Buddha abandoned his family to undertake the search that led to enlightenment, so Jesus rejected the ancient clan divisions in favor of a new order, a rejection he elaborates on in a variety of ways, here in Matthew 12:46–48:

> While Jesus was still talking to the crowd, his mother and brothers stood outside, wanting to speak to him. Someone told him, "Your mother and brothers are standing outside, wanting to speak to you."
>
> He replied to him, "Who is my mother, and who are my brothers?" Pointing to his disciples, he said, "Here are my mother and my brothers. For whoever does the will of my Father in heaven is my brother and sister and mother."

Jesus is saying—and Welty echoing—that the very survival of the species depends on our transcending ties based on blood and marriage—the ties of the Chisoms, the ties of blood and clan which perpetrate and reinforce conflict—recognizing instead the bonds of love, with friendship, not marriage, as the tie that binds.

From the first, Welty writes of the challenges faced by the joyous heart, living among people who lack sensitivity or who, having possessed it in youth, are taught or teach themselves to let it go. In "Innisfallen" she writes, "You must never betray pure joy—the kind you were born and began with—either by hiding it or parading it in front of people's eyes; they didn't want to be shown it." Welty's observation brings to mind a poem by Emily Dickinson:

Why—do they shut Me out of Heaven?
Did I sing—too loud?

[#248]

"I don't know why people marry at all," Welty wrote to her first great love, a largely epistolary relationship that extended over many years—though Welty followed him to San Francisco before the man decamped to Europe with his boyfriend. For so many of Welty's characters, marriage is the "lowly thing" (Marianne Moore again) of satisfaction. What interested Welty—what she lived out—was the "pure thing" of joy.

Therein lies the answer to that precocious Stanford undergraduate's question. I revisit Welty's description of herself and her character Miss Eckhart as "exposing [themselves] to risk." She dedicated herself to the ideal of art over the compromise of marriage; to be vulnerable not to a particular individual but to the whole world. Was this by circumstance or by choice? The answer, revealed in her correspondence and her work, is surely and simply "yes" and "yes."

Welty had a later, very specific love: Ken Millar, a mystery writer who published as Ross MacDonald. Theirs is among the greatest of epistolary loves. In 1966, Welty, a fan of thrillers, sent Millar a note praising his fiction and enclosing—in her first communication—"The Mountaintop Prayer":

> Restore all for me in beauty,
> Make beautiful all that is before me,
> Make beautiful all that is behind me,
> Make beautiful my words.
> It is done in beauty.
> It is done in beauty.
> It is done in beauty.
> It is done in beauty.

She was fearless in her epistolary intimacy.

She and Millar maintained an active correspondence for many years, through traumas on both sides. They did not meet in person until 1971, when, unbeknownst to each other, they both stayed at New York's Algonquin Hotel. After their chance encounter in the lobby, they walked midtown Manhattan together, as much in love as any two people might be. Millar flew back to his home in California the next day, leaving a note for Welty at the Algonquin desk that concluded, "Meanwhile there are letters." Later he wrote from California, "Love and friendship are surely the best things in life and may . . . persist beyond life . . . like the light from a star so immeasurably distant that it can't be dated and questions of past and future are irrelevant. The source of the starlight may well be thought to be inside us, and we take credit for the forces that sustain us, as being loved makes us feel loveable . . . it's as if you stopped time and handed me a glass which admits the future to our present vision, and the past too, joining present and future times, as if we had lived beyond life . . ."

I note his invocation of the timelessness of time; the reality of the quantum physicist and of the artist and the writer and the lover: all moments are present to this moment. I feel the intimacy of their epistolary love, established and maintained not in the bedroom but through the blessed device of the post.

And so Welty reveals to me why, well into midlife, I am writing this book. To write it is to accomplish the journey that she, along with Whitman and Dickinson, accomplished; to accept the lesson offered by their lives and work; to accept that I am among this tribe of solitaries, whose destiny is to live alone, and to give and receive passion and love through means other than the literal. Spinsterhood is a calling. Bachelorhood is a legitimate vocation.

Welty was a genteel liberal in a violent place in a violent time. Like many of the great Southern white writers who stayed in the South, she was an advocate of change at a leisurely pace, the privileged stance satirized by Nina Simone in "Mississippi Goddam," in which the musicians in her band chant "Too slow!" as Simone sings counterpoint, "That's just the trouble." That Welty loved the human condition in all its diversity is evident from her stories and her photographs. That she was unable to rise farther above her time and place—well, I pull my forelock in respect and humility before the shaping hand of time and place. It is possible to admire "Powerhouse," her fictionalized portrait of Fats Waller—among her white contemporaries, only fellow Southerner and solitary James Agee wrote as knowledgeably

and lovingly about music and musicians—and at the same time to
wince when she compares Powerhouse to a monkey.

Racism was never simple. Maybe what has gone away since Welty's time is the willingness or capacity of many black people to for-
give in the measure white people required of them to live in a white
society. In any case, one characteristic links Phoenix Jackson, the
grandmother of "The Worn Path," braving the long walk through
the woods and the condescension and disdain of white men to seek
treatment for her grandson, with Laurel, the daughter of bourgeois
Jackson who has gone and stayed north: they are both solitaries.

Welty's Jackson garden is devoted most prominently to a collection
of hybrid roses carefully labeled with their names and years of introduction (e.g., "Antoine Rivoire 1895"). But its central feature is a
plaque installed after her death, featuring a quotation from a letter
she wrote in 1941, early in her career, to her agent, Diarmuid Russell.

> Every evening when the sun is going down and it is cool
> enough to water the garden, and it is all quiet except for the
> locusts in great waves of sound, and I stand still in one place
> for a long time putting water on the plants, I feel something
> new—that is all I can say—as if my will went out of me, as if
> I had a stubbornness and it was melting. . . . It is a real shock,
> because I had no idea that there had been in my life any rigid-
> ity or refusal or anything so profound, but the sensation is one
> of letting in for the first time what I believed I had already
> felt—in fact suffered from—a sensitivity to all that was near

or around. But this is different and frightening—no, not really frightening—because for instance when I feel without ceasing every change in the garden itself, the changes of light as the atmosphere grows darker, and the springing up of a wind, and the rhythm of the locusts, and the colors of certain flowers that become very moving—they all seem to be a part of some happiness or unhappiness, and unhappiness that is lost or left unknown or undone perhaps—and no longer simple in their beautiful but outward way. And the identity of the garden itself is lost. This probably sounds confused and I am, but it is not. The intensity is very great, it is too much not to regard seriously, and to try to understand and even be glad for . . .

"Letting in for the first time what I believed I had already felt—in fact suffered from—a sensitivity to all that was near or around." My mother found that experience in her sacred space, her greenhouse. She fed family and guests from the vegetable garden, but that was my father's territory; for my mother the garden represented work, nonstop work in a hot August kitchen, canning tomatoes and peaches and beets and green beans and ever more tomatoes. Her love she reserved for flowers—ephemeral, impractical, gorgeous.

She favored orchids and cactus—the most interesting plants. The kitchen table always featured a bouquet gathered from her flowerbeds, and it was through those, along with the eternally recycling liturgical calendar of the Roman Catholic church, that I learned to understand time as an illusion. Japonica, hyacinth, forsythia, jonquils, iris, dogwood, peonies, Easter lilies, honeysuckle, roses, day lilies, daisies, naked ladies, geraniums, obedient plant, chrysanthemums, nandina (sadly, invasive), American holly, Foster holly, English holly, glossy green-black magnolia leaves . . . the experienced gardener will read in this list poem a progression from spring through summer and autumn and into winter. When the monastery closed its greenhouse, she collected cymbidium orchid cuttings and grew these in abundance, fashioning their extravagant blossoms into corsages for family and town weddings, proms, and graduations. She made her interest in cacti known, with the result that every traveler to deserts brought back cuttings. Most exotic was the night-blooming cereus; on the evening it produced a bud, she gathered neighbors and family to watch into the night as it opened its delicate, grand, showy, evanescent display.

I have wondered if our mystics—and is Welty's letter not a testimonial of a mystical experience?—virtually all of whom were solitaries, might share a physiological trait. If neuroscientists were to conduct careful autopsies of such individuals, might they discover a greater concentration of nerve endings or denser parts of the brain, which could offer a physiological explanation for the state Welty so eloquently describes, and that I hear echoed in Henry James's memories of his childhood New York *flâneries,* or Zora Neale Hurston's childhood visions, or in Jean Renoir's description of Cézanne at his canvas, or Rabindranath Tagore adrift on a canoe in the Ganges Delta? Most of us postmoderns come close to that hypnagogic state only in the moments between sleep and waking, or through psychotropic drugs, if we experience it at all.

If this conception seems fanciful, compare Welty's vision, preserved on a plaque in her garden, to Thomas Merton's revelation in 1958, recorded in his *Conjectures of a Guilty Bystander* and preserved on a state historical plaque at the site in downtown Louisville:

At the corner of Fourth and Walnut, in the center of the shopping district, I was suddenly overwhelmed with the realization that I loved all those people, that they were mine and I theirs, that we could not be alien to one another even though we were total strangers. It was like waking from a dream of separateness, of spurious self-isolation in a special world, the world of renunciation and supposed holiness. . . . if only everybody could realize this! But it cannot be explained. There is no way of telling people that they are all walking around shining like the sun.

Writing on this quiet, hot summer morning in Tucson, I understand Welty's perception of being one with her garden and Merton's perception of being one with all those people "walking around shining like the sun" as being rooted in some essential, visceral way in their embrace of solitude. At the most literal level, if either Welty, in her garden, or Merton, on a busy city corner, had been with a companion, he or she would have been conversing with or listening to or being distracted by that companion and so would not have had the experiences they report. But what I'm writing about arises from some deeper place—a place built slowly, imperceptibly, unconsciously from hours and days and weeks and years of silence and solitude, whether alone with one's self or alone in a crowd. And what is the foundation of that place? With Merton and Welty, I think it is love—self-love—the heresy of self-love.

Why "heresy"? What was the critic and solitary Paul Zweig invoking in the title of his book-length meditation *The Heresy of Self-Love: A Study of Subversive Individualism*? Most obviously, the solitary is characterized as selfish—unwilling to take on the responsibilities (marriage, children) of a selfless life. This canard persists, even though in my experience it is solitaries who educate children or care for them in emergency rooms or care for and visit the elderly in facilities where they are seldom visited by their biological children or relatives.

John Keats taught us that genius lies in the capacity to hold in the heart two apparently contradictory ideas without striving after their resolution: to love the self, lose the self. "No self!" Suzuki Roshi would cry. He did not mean that we have no identities or responsibilities; rather he meant that wisdom locates the self in a continual process of giving it away, a truth Jesus also expressed.

This is an act of great courage, entailing openness and vulnerability and forgiveness and ever and always paying attention. These qualities, summed up in the now-familiar Buddhist term "mindfulness," are in scarce supply at any time but especially in our wired, fast-paced age, in which cheapness and convenience have replaced care and attention as our top priorities. To care enough to risk paying attention—to pull out the earplugs and take off the sunglasses and listen and look—how challenging is that. Knowing I will never reach that place, all the same I can admire it, aspire to it—the forested mountain on the horizon, beckoning me onward, where at the summit I will perceive all of us, every one, walking around shining like the sun.

CHAPTER 8

The Lover of God

Rabindranath Tagore

BORN IN 1861, Rabindranath Tagore, the first non-European to receive, in 1913, the Nobel Prize in Literature, was the thirteenth and last surviving child of a distinguished Bengali family, the youngest child of the previous generation's oldest child. I attribute Tagore's reputation as an "old soul" in part to this fact of genealogy, since, as the youngest of a vast clan, he would have grown up hearing, as I grew up hearing, family stories reaching far into the past. In the course of researching a Bengali character for a novel, I was drawn into Tagore's life through our shared experience as repositories of generations of memory and by his frequently and eloquently expressed awareness of his essential solitude.

Mahatma Gandhi called Rabindranath Tagore "Great Sentinel" and "Gurudev" ("divine mentor"). Tagore returned the favor by being among the first to call Gandhi "Mahatma" ("venerable"). Westerners lionize Gandhi, Tagore's contemporary, as the liberator of the subcontinent. But contemporary India, in her role as one of the world's leading software developers, owes as much to Tagore, champion of education, as to Gandhi, whose campaign of nonviolence did little to promote education. Thanks in part to the 1982 Hollywood block-buster film, the activist Gandhi is a common reference point world-wide, whereas in America, the contemplative and solitary Tagore is largely forgotten. But in Bangla, the world's seventh most commonly spoken language, Tagore's life and work remain the focus of aca-demic studies, even as street people in Kolkata (formerly Calcutta) and farmers in the remote villages of Bengal sing his songs and recite his poetry. Tagore might have his closest Western analogue in Bob Dylan, who along with Tagore is the only musician to receive the Nobel in literature.

From a letter from Tagore to his secretary:

I carry an infinite space of loneliness around my soul through which the voice of my personal life very often does not reach my friends—for which I suffer more than they do. I have my yearning for the personal world as much as any other mortal, or perhaps more. But my destiny seems to be careful that in my life's experiences I should only have the touch of person-ality and not the ties of it. All the while she [destiny] claims my thoughts, my dreams and my voice, and for that, detach-ment of life and mind is needed. In fact, I have constantly been deprived of opportunities for intimate [long-lasting] attachments of companionship. Then again I have such an extreme delicacy of sensitiveness with regard to personal relationship that even when I acknowledge and welcome it I cannot invite it to the immediate closeness of my life. This deficiency I acknowledge with resignation knowing that it is a sacrifice claimed of me by my Providence for some purpose which he knows.

On the announcement of the Nobel, newspapers in Britain and America hastened to assure their audiences that, though dark-skinned, Tagore was "genetically Aryan." In his Nobel, and the rush of the leading male Anglo poets of the day (W. B. Yeats, Ezra Pound) to promote it, I perceive the desire of the European literary world to laud this dark-skinned colonial so long as he accommodated their ideas of how a colonial should behave and write. When he proved to have projects of his own—among them, promoting Indian independence—the British literary world turned on him and his popularity plummeted.

On every European and American visit, Tagore met the leading intellectuals and artists of the time, and while some expressed skepticism, most were charmed and seduced. That Tagore was ethereally handsome and, judging from photographs, a ringer for a modern-day Jesus reinforced the English myth of a Bengali sage. Western intellectuals were eager for a scrim onto which to project their fantasies of an ancient wisdom which might revitalize or replace the materialism of Western society, with its bustle and noise and profit-driven destruction of the natural world. Tagore was held up as the personification of the ideal—advocated by Emerson, advanced by Whitman in *Leaves of Grass*, and given voice in Thoreau—of a merger of Western empiricism and Asian mysticism, an ideal Tagore embraced until the carnage of World War I and the rising tide of Indian nationalism strengthened his commitment to home rule.

That some Anglos changed their points of view from lionization to cynicism offers evidence less of Tagore's shortcomings, though there were many, than of their disappointment at finding he was not, after all, the Second Coming they had fantasized. Tagore's Nobel came about in part because the Nobel committee—in those days a profoundly conservative body which understood its mission as the cultivation and dissemination of Western European culture—had read little more than *Gitanjali* (*Song Offerings*), a modest collection of devotional poems celebrating the waterscape, villages, and deities of Tagore's beloved Ganges Delta and the only work of Tagore's then available in English. Tagore himself had translated *Gitanjali* from the original Bangla, with assistance from William Butler Yeats, who was also its principal promoter to the Nobel committee. The origins of the initially warm resonance between Tagore and Yeats are easy to perceive; both were poets from colonized lands where English dominated but whose cultures rooted themselves in their native tongues; both poets held strong home rule sentiments and would become anticolonial activists. In 1906, long before the Nobel Prize, Tagore had published "Amar Sonar Bangla" as a rallying cry for opponents of Lord Curzon's partition, part of the British Empire–wide strategy of divide and rule. His song "Bande Mataram" became the informal anthem of the Indian nationalist movement. Later, his "Jana Gana Mana" was chosen as the anthem of the new nation of India, and later still "Amar Sonar Bangla" revived as the anthem for the new nation of Bangladesh, making him the only composer of two national anthems.

Drawn by his powerful novels and essays, by some wordless, deep recognition of a fellow solitary, and by a lifelong fascination with Bengal, I traveled halfway around the world in search of Jorasanko, the Kolkata compound in which Tagore was born and where he died.

Built by the British Empire as its base for raping the subcontinent, Kolkata, "City of Joy," went in the course of the twentieth century from being Asia's wealthiest city to being its poorest. Here the forces and tragedies of capitalism and colonialism are laid bare: a throng of people, more humanity than the spacious, airy Western imagination can comprehend, whole villages on the broad sidewalks, cooking, sleeping, laughing, defecating, begging, nursing, and always and everywhere selling, selling, selling; and amid the infinite grada- tions of brown complexions that constitute Bengal, a solitary Anglo man a head taller than the swirling, eddying, singing, shouting, cha- otic mass. I am that man, that solitary, all but unique during the weeks of my visit—Anglos are not fond of visiting the scenes of our crimes—a white man traveling alone.

I meet local doctors, a husband and wife whose son would like to immigrate to the United States. The wife receives me in the visitors' parlor. She and her husband pursued their medical education in Mos- cow; they have traveled to London. She has an unmarried daughter of an eligible age. Within moments of our meeting she asks if I am married. Prepared for this question by friends and wanting no mis- understandings, I tell her I'm a gay man. She ponders. "I have heard of this phenomenon," she says.

Later she asks, is it not obvious that marriages arranged by par- ents are more likely to succeed than those arising from passion? Later she asks, is it not obvious that a man has three responsibilities: to marry, to give his wife children, preferably sons, and to support her while she raises them and later in her old age? Later she asks, is it not obvious that, when a man reaches a certain age, for the well- being of all concerned he should leave the household and the family to the women and retire in solitude, like an old tiger, to the forest?

Later she asks, of course we know men have sex with men, but why do you have to talk about it?

The struggle of people to maintain dignity in the most appalling environments; the exuberance, love of life, joy, city of joy, in conditions the prosperous would find unbearable.

I tremble for my race when I think that God is just.

I am searching for Jorasanko, home of the Tagores.

At the Kali temple: bloody mouth, necklace of skulls, black complexion. Baskets of scarlet hibiscus, to feed her appetite for blood; flocks of goats, sacrificed hourly, to feed her appetite for blood. It was, I believe, this cultural familiarity with death—the perception of it not as the termination of life but as life's essential and ever-present complement—that led Tagore to think on it so deeply; Elisabeth Kübler-Ross opens every chapter of her groundbreaking *On Death and Dying* with quotations from his writing.

The great festival is underway, celebrating Durga, patroness of Kolkata, virgin and mother of Shiva's children, and her defeat of the evil demon Mashisha: pandals larger than mansions, larger than palaces, bamboo framing covered with hemp woven into fantastic architectural detail, woven into animals and humans and pilasters and Corinthian columns and rosettes and featuring in every interior, as unvarying as the ox and lamb and Virgin and babe of the Christmas crèche, variations on the goddess Durga, solitary warrior, astride her lion, her four children to either side, a weapon in each of her ten arms and in one hand the trident with which she pierces the blue demon Mashisha at her feet, in his manifestation as a water buffalo.

A fantasy city built in the architecture of dreams, built to be destroyed. People crowd the puja pandals. A great pandal dedicated to Muhammad Ali, with a banner over its entrance, "A LIFE WITHOUT FEAR." On the last day the city parades to the river and returns the goddesses to their origins, mud to mud; there is no past, no future, time is an illusion, there is only here and now, let us begin and begin and begin again.

The monsoons have prolonged themselves but in my very Anglo determination to make use of every moment, I set out to find Jorasanko.

Rain falls steadily. In a city with little drainage, the streets are knee-deep in water. Only the skinny rickshaw drivers are at work, pulling their fares through the flooded streets. The Russian-built metro arrives and departs precisely on time. I get off near the Asia Society, club and home base for remaining members of the upper castes that aligned themselves with the Raj. Surely someone there will direct me to Jorasanko? The entrance is manned by four armed guards, smoking. I ask for directions to Jorasanko. The guard requests my passport. He inspects every page, including the blank pages, then hands it to his fellow guard, who repeats the inspection. All four guards inspect it, then the last vanishes through a door, my passport in hand. They indicate a bench. I wait. An hour passes. "All I want are directions to Jorasanko," I say. The guards smile. I wait. They smoke. I wait. After another hour, in desperation I pull a business card from my wallet. "I'm a professor," I say. "May I have my passport?" The first guard inspects my card, then hands it to the second, who hands it to the third, who inspects it and says, "The distinguished professor from America! You must meet the director!" "But I don't want to meet the director," I say. "I just want my passport." I've given up on the day's project of locating Jorasanko. The rain is still falling. "You must meet the Society director, when he returns from tea," the first guard says. "And when will he return from tea?" I ask. The guard smiles. An hour passes. The fourth guard returns, carrying my passport. "The director is happy to make an appointment," he says. "But I don't want to see the director," I say. My passport disappears again. A half hour passes. At 4 p.m. the guard returns. "Your appointment with the director is at 5 p.m.," he says. "May I have my passport?" I ask, figuring that, with it in hand, I will make a break for the door. "After your appointment with the director," he says. An hour passes. Precisely at 5 p.m. the guard beckons me forward.

The director's office is on the top floor, an ornate room with high ceilings and vast paintings from centuries of European colonialism. Mold covers one wall and creeps over the paintings. The director waves me to a seat. He sits at his empty, spotless desk. "The distinguished professor of English," he says. "I'm not that kind of professor," I respond. "Actually, I'm just looking for Jorasanko," and in his slight grimace the thought occurs that Tagore was most likely no friend of the Asia Society, that just possibly I am being given the runaround. Then he smiles and places his hands together and stands. "'The Prelude,'" he says, "by William Wordsworth," and recites from memory, ten minutes and more. His hands come together again and he sits. "Now you must recite for me," he says. "Shelley? Byron?" "I'm afraid I don't memorize the British," I say. "You must give a lecture," he says. "Really, you are so kind," I say, "but I just came to find Jorasanko, and so if I could have my passport returned . . ." "We will arrange a date," he says, pulling out his calendar. "Next Thursday," he says, "at noon. I will invite our board. They will be so pleased to hear from the distinguished visiting professor from America." "I don't have a lecture prepared," I say. "I didn't travel with any notes." "Your topic?" he asks. "Well, I just wrote a book on the encounter of

Buddhism and Christianity in America," I say. He frowns. "I must consult with my board."

Back-and-forth for several minutes, while the painting molders and the rains continue. Finally I am released, and oh, yes, your passport, a matter of no consequence, ask downstairs. And I ask downstairs, and my passport is produced, and I am shown the door.

When I emerge—the end of the day now, a day on which I had a long list of projects—I am learning not to make lists of projects, I am learning to submit, I am learning about life in Kolkata, I am learning about life—the rains have stopped. I wade through flooded streets, back to the subway, back to the rickshaw, back to the Vedantist study center where I am staying—an institute founded by followers of Brahmo Samaj, a monotheistic reformist movement of Hinduism cofounded by Tagore's father. The moment I enter my cell, the telephone, which has not been working and which will never work again, rings. The director of the Asia Society is calling. "No American will be allowed to speak on Buddhism," he says. "Another topic, please."

I'm sullen. "Memoir," I say. "I write memoir. I can talk about writing memoir." He rings off.

I spend the intervening week wondering if I dreamed this day or if in fact I am obligated to appear, but I, ever the polite visitor and, it must be said, curious what adventure waits, show up at the appointed time. There, in the bright, hot, humid midday sun of Kolkata, on the sidewalk packed with street vendors and beggars and bureaucrats in dhotis on their midday break and the unbreathable air and din of passing lorries, a skeletally thin man with a pronounced limp is walking up and down, up and down, wearing a sandwich board reading *Fenton Johnson / Distinguished American Professor / Lectures on Wordsworth / 12:00.*

In the upstairs conference room: forty solemn women wearing gorgeously patterned silk saris and one handsome man. The director introduces me. I give a brief summary of the concept of a creative writing program and my place in it. I read from my memoir of my partner who died of AIDS in Paris in 1990, pages of which I had located online and printed in an internet café. When I say the word AIDS, the director rises and leaves. I speak of my conversation with the one person charged with administering AIDS prevention programs in Kolkata, a city of fifteen million. The women are stone-faced. I invite questions. There are no questions. The handsome man presents me with a bouquet of roses and an honorarium: 500 rupees, about four dollars. How might I find Jorasanko? I ask. He brings his hands together, bows, and smiles.

Rabindranath Tagore understood his formative setting to be not the congested streets of Kolkata but rural Bengal, the great delta of the Ganges, where life patterns were shaped not by land but by water: the annual, harmonic rhythm of monsoon floods, planting, and harvests, and the religious festivals celebrating these. Though educated in Jorasanko, Tagore spent much of his adulthood as the benevolent overseer of the villages of the family's Ganges Delta estates, a role richly portrayed in *The Home and the World*, Bengali director Satyajit Ray's lush film adapted from Tagore's novel of the same name. Though Tagore was caught up in the social and cultural upheaval that marked the emergence of India in the twentieth century, he was first and foremost a chronicler of village life, in song, poetry, prose, theater, and painting.

Writing at the time of the building of the modern nation-state of India from humankind's most ancient surviving culture, Tagore ceaselessly experimented with old forms of music and poetry. Though he never played a musical instrument, he composed some two thousand songs. His collected works fill thirty-two volumes. Late in life he took up painting, exhibiting in major cities around the world. He opposed all forms of militarism, and protested the British firing on Sikh pilgrims at Amritsar in 1919 by disavowing the knighthood Britain had conferred on him. And yet he could also oppose Swadeshi, Mahatma Gandhi's program of self-reliance, on the basis that it created a barrier between England and India, Hindu and Muslim, when, in his view, cooperation, collaboration, and education were the only roads to peaceful coexistence.

His commitment to education was lifelong and unwavering. He founded first a utopian school at Shantiniketan, where his father had already established an ashram for Brahmo Samaj. Later Tagore *fils* enlarged his school into a utopian university, Visva-Bharati, which played a major role in the maturation of some of the greatest artists and thinkers of the new Indian nation, among them Satyajit Ray and the Nobel-winning economist Amartya Sen.

But Tagore always understood the arts and the sciences, East and West, mysticism and reason, as inseparable and symbiotic. Abroad he defended Indian spirituality; in India he defended the Western enshrinement of reason.

In this he revealed another characteristic my solitaries share: he was ornery, a contrarian, one who turned over the stone of received opinion to find the riches underneath. Tagore was utterly committed to the beauty and power of reason even as he understood that reason was only one aspect of the great harmonic chorus of the universe—

the conductor, perhaps, to sustain the entirely apt metaphor, first-rank in importance, but not to be confused with the music itself. His achievements were the fruit of aristocratic privilege, but the dominant motif of his life was simplicity and solitude.

As a youth—as one might expect of the thirteenth and youngest child of a vast clan deeply invested in its intellectual and aesthetic traditions—Tagore became fascinated with poetry from earlier times. At the age of fourteen he wrote eight poems in a distinctive lyrical style dating from the sixteenth century, celebrating the unrequited love of the maiden Radha for her lord Krishna. Claiming that he had found and copied the poems from an ancient manuscript, Tagore presented them to his older brother, editor of a literary journal underwritten by the family. The brother was much taken with their beauty and accepted them immediately. When Tagore revealed the deception, his brother delighted in the joke, eventually publishing thirteen of his youngest brother's poems under the title *The Lover of God* and the pseudonym Bhanusimha Thakur.

The poems might be dismissed as an adolescent prank, but in them Tagore, disguised from others and, most intriguingly, from himself, assumes the persona of a middle-aged lady-in-waiting advising the young princess Radha on matters of the heart. He anticipates Virginia Woolf's praise of androgyny as the foundation of creativity; in the manner of Jane Austen, Henry James, or Eudora Welty, the solitary occupies the role of gender-ambiguous sage and counselor regarding relationships.

Perhaps in imitation of Whitman, whose *Leaves of Grass* Tagore greatly admired, Tagore added to and revised those early poems throughout his life. For many years he denied his authorship of them; at one point, to underscore the joke, he authored a fake biography of the fake poet, written in the high academic style he detested.

However fantastically overcrowded and polluted, India has not banished its gods and goddesses. Today you still find them hanging out casually on every street, in every village lane, in the subway stations, in the rice paddies. Every corner tree and lightpost features a tiny altar to some member of the Hindu panoply of deities; they inhabit Tagore's every poem. I open my copy of *The Lover of God* randomly, to encounter immediately references to Kala, goddess of art, and Kānu, a diminutive of Lord Krishna.

> You listen, Kānu, Divine Lord among beasts,
> she thirsts for the pure nectar of your love.
> Let her drink.

As is statistically demonstrable with youngest sons, Tagore may have carried a genetic predisposition to androgyny or, perhaps, an unexpressed homosexuality—I'm thinking of the poems of *The Lover of God* and the organic ease with which, as a fourteen-year-old, Tagore inhabited a woman's consciousness. Poems by a fourteen-year-old, late-nineteenth-century Bengali boy, dreaming himself into the persona of a middle-aged duenna, three centuries in the past, advising her lady on her romantic obsession with a god; poems the boy, later a Nobel laureate, revisited and revised until he was nearly eighty years old.

I find a gentle lesson here for our postmodern, materialist, secularized, fact- and device- and identity-obsessed West—a lesson about penetrating the baroque delights of the surface to the essential unity (Brahma) of what lies underneath, with the self not as a fixed entity but a door waiting to be opened to a hallway of mirrors framing more doors, each to be opened and explored, in solitude and in silence.

In his reminiscences, Tagore makes only passing reference to his marriage, arranged in 1883 to a child bride ten years old; Tagore was twenty-two. He and his wife lived together only briefly; she died in 1902. In his memoir he writes a single sentence, "I was married"; that is the sum of his assessment. Though Tagore spoke against child marriage, he arranged for his daughters to marry at ten and fifteen years of age—perhaps, one of his biographers speculates, to free himself for his life projects, the schools at Shantiniketan and Visva-Bharati. At the time of his favorite daughter's death from tuberculosis, Tagore had hardly seen her in five years. Like Whitman—like me—Tagore wrote of an idealized companion. "If only, right now, someone dear to me were here, one human companion I could love," he wrote in his short story "The Postmaster." His child bride could not fill that role, whether because of limitations on her part or because her upbringing had not provided her the slightest preparation to be other than a submissive, not-seen-and-not-heard, sequestered-in-purdah wife.

To provide context for Tagore's misogyny as well as a sobering reminder of the cultural norms of early-twentieth-century India even among educated men, I note that Gandhi treated women with comparable indifference, in marked contrast to, e.g., Walt Whitman and Henry David Thoreau, with Whitman in particular repeatedly including and celebrating the place of women in the great American experiment of democracy. That neither Tagore nor Gandhi overcame this elemental prejudice speaks volumes about the weight of Bangla and Hindu tradition and the liberation that arose, at least for some, in North America, the new, relatively unencumbered continent, where women were, if not equals, at least necessary partners in the settlement and exploitation of the land and its native peoples. And though Tagore took care to differentiate between the rigid social structures of the Hindu caste system and his Brahmin ideals, he never repudiated the privilege his caste afforded him. One of his biographers characterizes him as "an aristocrat not a democrat," and in fact Shantiniketan segregated Brahmin from non-Brahmin boys from its founding in 1901 until the 1915 visit by Gandhi, who was not Brahmin.

And yet: writers and artists form and express their most foundational truths in and through their work. Tagore's poetry and prose, including most notably *The Home and the World*, reveal a tender and profound sensitivity to the awakening expectations and trials of women in a rapidly changing India. In this he was among the voices—he was perhaps *the* great literary voice—paving the way for his fellow Bengali Bharati Mukherjee's *The Middle Passage and Other Stories*, which received the National Book Award in Fiction in 1984 and opened the floodgates for the current wealth of writing by women of the subcontinent.

In Shantiniketan's initial years, the Kolkata elite dismissed Tagore's university as hopelessly idealistic, but one sees in its principles and in Tagore's vision the essence of the solitary's idealism—my father's secular monastery, if you will. Its founding required a certain faith in destiny. That the land on which it was built was a parched tract in a poverty-stricken region of Bengal hardly mattered, since, for Tagore the mystic, the mind could make a heaven of any hell. Satyajit Ray, who lived there from 1940 to 1942, recalled it as "a world of vast open spaces, vaulted over with a dustless sky, that on a clear night showed the constellations as no city sky could ever do . . . if Shantiniketan did nothing else, it induced contemplation, and a sense of wonder, in the most prosaic and earthbound of minds." Tagore emphasized the character of the place and its commitment to solitaries and solitude in a letter to his niece: "far horizons, black storm-clouds and profound feelings—in other words, where infinitude is manifest—are most truly witnessed by one person; a multitude makes them petty and distracting." In its early years Shantiniketan imposed a standard of living that was, depending on your point of view, ascetic or primitive, but as the land recovered from its abuses and responded to Tagore's reclamation projects, the school became a byword for the cultivation of beauty—that is, a theme and watchword for the solitary's project.

As the youngest of thirteen, Tagore would have had from earliest consciousness an intimate relationship with death, because he would have been looking on as one by one his elders died. In fact Tagore survived his wife, three children, five brothers, and three sisters. "This conviction appeared in my writing again and again," he wrote, "that it is in the form of sorrow and despair, conflict and death that the infinite makes its appearance in life." Earlier he writes, "In order to know life as real one has to make its acquaintance through death. . . . The person who rushes ahead to take death a captive can see that what he seizes on is not death, it is life."

Death . . .
I shall welcome, and receive him
with my whole heart, and believe him
friend and soulmate dear . . .

Tagore, Gitanjali

. . . to die is different from what any one supposed, and
    luckier.

Whitman, Leaves of Grass

And so midway through my month in Kolkata I take the train to
Benares, city of death, where orthodox Hindus come to die because,
in the Hindu cosmology, to die in Benares is to escape the karmic
cycle of life and death and pass directly to nirvana. Bengali friends
wisely advised me to arrange for a guide. But my train arrived late
on a blisteringly hot day, I was feverish, and so, after waiting an hour
in the heat—not so much as a shade shelter at the train station—
and uneasy at drinking the little water that was to be had, I hired
a cab driver to penetrate the impenetrable maze of Benares. When
my guide arrived at my hotel an hour later—four hours later than
our appointment—I fired him, a stupid decision born of so many
cultural assumptions, chief among them my understanding of time
as governed by calendar and clock. Why arrive at the station "on
time" when the train arrives and departs on a schedule known only
to the gods? "I don't need a guide," I thought. "I can travel alone, I've
always traveled alone. I will learn it all by myself."

As indeed I did, but I recommend against this particular exercise in Western arrogance. A couple travels as a self-contained unit,
in which each serves as a sounding board and defender of the other;

the solitary is exposed and vulnerable before whatever adventure the journey presents. To offer the most explicit example: beggars and hawkers in the streets made a beeline for me, the solitary Anglo who had no obvious refuge, no one at hand to turn to so as to ignore the extended hand or the high-volume sales pitch.

The broad sweep of the Ganges. Hymns chanted in unison. In the narrow alleyway in front of the hotel a banyan tree raises its limbs over crowded houses, its roots flowing over broken walls and pavement seeking earth, its branches filled with spider monkeys silhouetted against the last light from the setting sun, their screeches and screams punctuating the sitar and flute and tabla from the burning ghats, where the smoke from today's cremations rises to become what is. The lowest caste rakes through the ashes for gold fillings or silver rings, their salary for tending to the untouchable dead. The bell stops. On the darkening river a flotilla of oil lamps drifts, set afloat by the faithful, each carrying a wish or a prayer. On the steps immediately below someone has just released the day's sewage, which flows down the steps to join Mother Ganga. A few feet from where the brown sewage dumps into the river, men and children are bathing. Some drink of the holy river, some brush their teeth. The ghats are lined with two-prowed skiffs that take people on the river. A spider monkey creeps along the ledge under my balcony, almost within touch; his big brown eyes and slightly worried gaze meet mine. Another flotilla of oil lamps slowly makes its way downriver. Another conch shell blows; the music steps up its rhythm. This is music meant to penetrate the heart and it is no wonder that the British held it in unease. Someone is ringing a bell, blowing a conch, banging a tin cymbal on the vast wide sweep of the bend in the river. The alleyways are at times narrow as my shoulders and never more than ten feet wide, a space shared by goats, cattle with calves, vendors, children, bicycles, the occasional motorbike, mangy dogs, cow pies, monkeys. Teams of men from the lowest caste, dressed in white, the color of death, carry the dead on pallets on their shoulders, marching double-time; the crowds part as if by magic to let them pass as they convey the corpses to the burning ghats. Ascetics of all persuasions wander through; emaciated men and women who have come here to die wander through. Someone is always at my elbow to offer post-cards, a massage, beer, hash, opium, girls, boys.

Near the burning ghats, five wooden platforms face the river. On each stands a young man dressed in white, edged with red or green. In coordinated choreography they face to one side, then to the river, then to the other side, waving first peacock-feather fans, then great dusters made of bound grasses. The movement is slow and graceful and hypnotic. The priest is chanting hymns over the loudspeakers while tabla, sitar, and flute play. Cattle wander through the crowd. The boats pull up one by one, the pilgrims debark. A saffron-robed monk wanders through the crowd with sacred fire cupped in a clay saucer; people wave their hands over it. After an hour the dancers stop but the conch shells blow and bells ring into the night.

The next day I meet with a devout scholar of Sanskrit, a lifelong solitary who has come to Benares to die. She serves me tea in her tiny apartment, where she is watching American Christian cable. From my notes:

- A Jew or a Muslim is made a Jew or a Muslim through cir-cumcision, a Christian is made a Christian through bap-tism, but we are born Hindu.
- When you worship you become the deity. Incense symbol-

izes purification by fire; you are burning the five senses, you are surrendering everything.

- The river is the microcosmic self, the ocean is the macrocosmic self. The soul flows down from the mountain to join its larger self. Once you are in the river, you are bound to reach your destination. It's not water, it's energy. Good and evil are the play of language, nothing else. Language is maya which you have to forget in order to experience what lies beyond.

- If good comes into your life, it's because you've been blessed by God, not because you're better than others.

- Good and evil are the same thing—the same person in different masks. We meditate at dusk or dawn because that's when good mixes with evil, light with dark. I do not concern myself with what is good, what is evil. I concern myself with right action. In what way may I be in accord with the moment—to do what it asks of me? Americans want direct action, but direct action is seldom the best means to the goal. Patience is what is called for, to let the matter reveal itself for what it is.

- We will burn the homosexuals.

- The universe is a bright jewel set firm in forgiving and held fast by love.

- A rain of flowers accompanies a great hero's death.

Men with gold or metallic white or silver or red paint on their foreheads, marks of their particular devotion. Drums beating, low- and high-pitched bells ringing, gongs, chanting, past and through the burning bodies, the minor key colors—ochre, tan, sandstone—of the temples and ghats lit by the light off the river, the stench of sewage, the splash of pilgrims and old men bathing, the water, the devotees of Shiva with red threads around their arms, the boat ride, the oars two bamboo trunks with boards nailed to them, the boatman older than time, a world outside of time or maybe without time. Time is an illusion. I confess I do not believe in time.

> There is no time, all past and all future
> is contained in this moment.
>
> Rabindranath Tagore, *Balai*

At each day's end I retreat to my cell and wonder: Did I really see that? Did that really happen? Questions rendered more piercing and unanswerable because I had no second pair of eyes, I had no companion, I traveled alone.

And yet who would want a companion as a scrim between oneself and India, between life and death? None of this would have happened to the coupled me. The solitary traveler occupies a place of openness that becomes a place of radical empowerment, because learning begins in letting go, becoming vulnerable, feeling awkward and stupid, losing the self to find the self.

For all his respect for science, knowledge, education, Tagore was at heart a contemplative. One reads it in his poetry, which idealizes the timeless cycle of rural life, with its rhythmic progression from one season to the next, each season with particular tasks to be performed in consonance with the demands of nature. Tagore's international travel deepened his contemplative nature; he encountered the environmental and social destruction of industrialization world-wide and, like any sensitive soul, was appalled. Perhaps that is why he advocated the slow, labor-intensive, one-mind-at-a-time approach to change.

In their 1995 biography *The Myriad-Minded Man*, Krishna Dutta and Andrew Robinson compared Tagore to Gandhi as a means of underscoring Tagore's role in Indian history. "Tagore versus Gandhi was the cherisher of beauty versus the ascetic; the artist versus the utilitarian; the thinker versus the man of action; the individualist versus the politician; the elitist versus the populist; the widely-read versus the narrowly-read; the modernist versus the reactionary; the believer in science versus the anti-scientist; the synthesizer of East and West versus the Indian chauvinist; the internationalist versus the nationalist; the traveler versus the stay-at-home; the Bengali versus the Gujarati; the scholarly Brahmin versus the merchant Vaishya; and, most prominently, the fine flowing robes and beard versus the coarse loincloth and bald pate."

In that list—as best I can tell from my research, not pejorative but merely descriptive—I search for my own place on the spectrum from mystic (Tagore) to pragmatist (Gandhi). It seems so predictable that the Brahmin Tagore, who grew up in a palace, however humbly appointed, underwritten by generations of collaboration with the British, should be the voice of liberal moderation, while Gandhi, born to the merchant class which had a problematic relationship with the British authorities, would become the voice of nonviolent revolution. Tagore was a solitary—"a boy who was shy and kept to himself, playing his solitary games," he wrote of himself, a "rogue" and "vagabond" with an inclination for breaking tradition, who at the same

time was passionately committed to the concept of nonduality—
of complete unity between the mind and soul. In *Tagore: A Life*,
Krishna Kripilani writes, "The basic and most robust characteristic
of Tagore's philosophy of life was . . . that there is no inherent contradiction between the claims of the so-called opposites—the flesh and
the spirit, the human and the divine, love of life and love of God, joy
in beauty and pursuit of truth, social obligation and individual rights,
respect for tradition and the freedom to experiment, love of one's
people and faith in the unity of mankind." In the end, I apply a lesson
from Hinduism: rather than see Gandhi and Tagore in opposition, I
see them as complementary—as night is to day, Tagore is to Gandhi,
the contemplative and thinker who articulates the foundation on
which the activist builds a nation. In assessing their misogyny, I try
mightily to remember that, as they were men of their times, I am
shaped by my historical moment—my fate—and that, if I am remembered, later generations will in their turn be bemused or horrified by
my blind spots, which by definition I cannot perceive. I reach back in
my life to recall as well a lesson I learned from a San Francisco Zen
Center gardener: "Aren't we fortunate that the teachings come to us
in flawed vessels."

Tagore was able to articulate and realize his vision in some significant measure because he was not bound by the demands of his
own wife and children, a fact he recognized. "I have clearly realized that God has not created me for a householder's life. I sup-
pose that is why . . . I have been constantly wandering about and

have never been able to establish a home anywhere . . ." The less praiseworthy side of Tagore's life—e.g., his indifference to his wife and children—offers evidence, perhaps, of what happens when the round peg of the solitary is forced into the square hole of conventional societal demands, or the conflict so many artists experience between their calling and their particular responsibilities: to spouses, to children, to family. I'm moved to consider that their families and lovers might have fared better had the rest of my solitaries followed the examples of Henry James and Eudora Welty and remained solo and childless.

I encounter his biographers' characterization of Tagore as "ferociously egocentric" and wonder if their characterization arises from horror at the heresy of self-love. If one teaches, as Tagore taught, that the individual is a microcosm of the world and that there is no separation between the individual and the world, the best way—indeed, the only way—to selfless generosity is through the fullest love of the self. That required Tagore to leave behind conventional family roles, as it had required the Buddha to leave his wife sleeping next to his newborn son to set out on his journey of self-discovery, and Jesus to claim as his true mother and brothers not his blood family but those who follow the will of God.

Tagore defined "sin" as "not one mere action but . . . an attitude of life which takes for granted that one's goal is finite, that our self is the ultimate truth, that we are not all essentially one but exist each for his own separate individual existence." By extension, virtue consists of merging the particular and individual into the communal, the universal, the enduring. Curious and significant, is it not, that this self-described solitary should so passionately advocate the unity of all creation. That, perhaps, is what defines the mystic: in the alembic of solitude, she or he compounds the fate of the individual and the fate of the cosmos into symbiosis.

The day after my adventure at the Asia Society, I hire a car and direct the driver to take me to Jorasanko. Stifling heat, steam rising from the broken pavements. For hours the car inches forward between people and goats and cows and lorries and more people. We move at the pace of a monk in walking meditation. I pay the driver and walk. I get lost.

Where is the cheerful man astride the elephant who with its trunk plucks the 100-rupee note from my pocket? Where is the woman panhandling with the battered hubcap and, at her feet, the limbless, twitching baby lying face down on the pavement? What is time? Illusion. What is death? Life.

The men holding hands. The plates of recycled cardboard and banana leaf on which street vendors sell their food. The smell of cooking in the streets; the smell of tuberoses and defecation and diesel exhaust in the streets. The community of hijras, self-castrated men who live below the overpasses as women. The people crowd around the Brahmin priest in white muslin as he sprinkles them with Ganges water using a stem of basil or places a handful of marigold and hibiscus petals into their outstretched hands. I return to the monastery, giddy from the heat.

I am still searching for Jorasanko.

Courtesy of the international secret decoder ring society through which LGBT travelers in closeted lands make contacts with locals,

I meet with Kolkata's nascent LGBT rights organization Swikriti, comprising six gay men and one fierce lesbian. On my last full day in Kolkata she invites me and her fellow activists to a midday meal at her parents' small apartment in Dum Dum, a suburb named for the explosions made by ordnance when the Raj used this area as an artillery testing ground. I am conscious of the resources my hosts have invested in this meal, conscious of my fantastic wealth and my height and breadth; I tower over everyone in the group, I have always had plenty to eat and space to grow and expand. The lesbian interprets for her grandfather, who tells me his story of surviving the Indian government massacre of the Naxalites, leftist Maoists whom the government of India is still trying to obliterate. During the bloody Bangladeshi war for independence in 1971, thousands were rounded up and shot. He escaped by pretending to be dead and, when dark fell, crawling to safety over his murdered comrades. The next day the corpses were bulldozed into a mass grave. Now the remaining Naxalites have retreated to the state of Assam, the remote northeast of India, the origin of the crafts Swikriti is selling to support their struggle for LGBT civil rights.

I am lightheaded with fever; I will barely reach Rome the next day before collapsing—less from illness, though there is that, than from sensory overload. I feel ignorant and inescapably American before another forgotten horror of history. They want me, the writer, to carry the Naxalite story to the world, but years have passed and this is the best I can do.

After lunch, they produce an assemblage of objects donated from the tribal corners of Assam. Thrifty traveler that I am, I have spent my rupees—when am I likely to be in India again?—and I have remaining only the equivalent of fifty American dollars. There is no place where a traveler may obtain cash in Dum Dum. I ask for a price; I want to be sure to exceed what they have paid and of course they smile and bow, they will never reveal to a guest what they paid. In the end I give them everything in my wallet, though back in America I look at the white linen cloth interwoven with gold thread draped across my sofa and I am seized with guilt that I acquired these objects—there were others—for less than they might have brought in a tourist market.

When we leave, we walk through alleys too narrow for a rickshaw. I ask, and they, my fellow queers, my fellow outsiders, take me to Jorasanko.

Jorasanko Thakur Bari, "House of the Tagores," the family compound in which Tagore grew up, is a multistory mansion surrounding a courtyard encircled by open-air porches on each floor—an architecture that walls off the external world while allowing for free circulation of light, air, and gossip. The guards ask for my passport and I show it but I do not let it leave my hands. The building is rather grand, with one wing once reserved for purdah. A few of Tagore's black-and-white brush paintings are on display, some labeled in Bangla—the government of West Bengal, still angry at the British, translates nothing into English.

In the courtyard—evening now—we encounter the reincarnation of Durga: a small girl chosen for characteristics that evoke the goddess (flat feet, a certain posture), dressed in scarlet silks and placed on a pedestal while the Brahmin priest in his white skirt sprinkles us with Ganges water as incense burns and the drummers beat a wild rhythm against the backdrop of Durga piercing the demon at her feet.

In my childhood, the first-grade class elected four boys who would be dressed in snappy sky-blue capes and would carry a statue of the Virgin along the town's single street in the May procession. The mothers made garlands of May flowers, peonies and spirea and early roses, and festooned the statue's palanquin, while parents and children followed the village priest, bedecked in a golden chasuble, chanting Latin. The chants return to me, *Salve Regina, rosa mystica, domus de aurum*, as I walk over the muddy, broken pavements outside the Tagore mansion, past the drivers huddling in the rickshaws, the tarps pulled down against an evening shower, past those drivers who have found a fare and are maneuvering their carts through the stream of cars and buses and trucks and people and cattle, immersed in this sea of diesel exhaust while a sari-clad woman, borne on a palanquin, holds herself upright on the seat like a queen—as the sidewalk vendors with their fruits and vegetables brightened by the wet approach her, their goods extended—the handsome teenage boys walking with their arms draped over each other's shoulders and everywhere kindness and cooperation and generosity, everywhere illness and deformity and death.

At the airport, I phone my mother, halfway around the world. She asks for my impressions of Kolkata, and without thinking I respond, "How stingy are people who have everything, how generous those who have nothing!"

In his dictated deathbed statement, Tagore said, "Today my sack is empty. I have given completely whatever I had to give." The statement recalls Eudora Welty—"What animates me and possesses me is . . . the love of . . . art and the love of giving it, the desire to give it until there is no more left"—or Henry James's "magnanimity," or Marianne Moore's "idealism willing to make sacrifices for its self-preservation." Each of these solitaries understood solitude as a vocation, a particular calling from an external force or destiny, our best means to give and give until there is no more left.

CHAPTER 9

A Soundless Island in a Tideless Sea

Zora Neale Hurston

MY MOTHER'S FAMILY HANDED down a cut-glass cruet. It was not crystal but it was old, and for any glass object, especially one in frequent usage, to survive so long is remarkable. It came, I believe, from my mother's great-grandmother. We used it for one purpose: it held cider vinegar, which we sprinkled over boiled greens. In France— for that matter, in other regions of America—a vinegar cruet would imply a mate to hold oil, but in our lives green salads were an affectation recently arrived from elsewhere, probably with the arrival of grocery stores with refrigerated produce flown in from California and marketing campaigns for bottled dressings. In my mother's kitchen, in my youth, I recall only one green salad, made with the crispest of lettuce (black-seeded Simpson) and diced green onions, both picked moments before and dressed with bacon grease hot from the skillet. Only the freshest lettuce would hold up to such heat, but as I write I hear the pop and sizzle of the hot grease dripped on the still-wet lettuce and my mouth waters for that dish peculiar to my childhood and, in my childhood, to my mother's kitchen.

About those boiled greens. Kale, always—we grew no other win-

ter green—picked that morning and put on the stove at noon with
a chunk of pork belly and a diced onion, cooked at a slow simmer
for five or six hours until supper, sprinkled with cider vinegar—the
cut-glass cruet makes its appearance—and served with cornbread
made using the coarse-ground meal appropriated (more theft) from
the great sacks delivered to the distillery for use in making bourbon mash. With her first bite, my mother announced, "These greens
are *tough*," a statement that had nothing to do with texture but was
instead an invitation for contradiction and compliment.

The cruet was deeply cut in a geometric pattern of diamonds
alternating with florets; my thumb easily recalls their nubbled glass.
Its stopper was round and hexagonally faceted. Of all kitchen objects
it most resonantly embodies my childhood in that vanished time and
culture, possibly because its use was so particular to a regional dish,
possibly because of its age, possibly because of its evocation of the
many ancestors, reaching deep into the nineteenth century, through
whose hands it had passed. Late spring evenings, the windows bright
with the low-slanting sun, and my ignorance and innocence of the
great world beyond the line of hills that enclosed and enveloped my
little town, the world that so thoroughly occupied my imagination,
into which I was, soon enough and in fulfillment of my dreams—be
careful what you pray for—to be thrown. The cut-glass cruet is for
me the synecdoche of my mother's family, the object that embodies
the whole. Among my solitaries, it most vividly brings to mind Zora
Neale Hurston, whose passion at times found its expression with men
and at other, equally significant times through "corn pone and mus-
tard greens, or rubbing a paragraph with a soft cloth."

African American novelist and pioneering anthropologist Zora
Neale Hurston understood her calling to solitude almost from the

moment she was conscious. In her memoir *Dust Tracks on a Road*—
the title could serve as a Buddhist koan—she describes her childhood vision of her future:

> I do not know when the visions began. Certainly I was not
> more than seven years old . . . I never told anyone around me
> about these strange [visions]. . . . they would laugh me off as
> a storyteller. Besides, I had a feeling of difference from my
> fellow men, and I did not want it to be found out. Oh, how I
> cried out to be just as everyone else! . . . When I was an ordi-
> nary child, and no knowledge of things but the life about me, I
> was reasonably happy. I would hope that the call would never
> come again. But even as I hoped, I knew that the cup meant
> for my lips would not pass. I must drink the bitter drink. I
> studied people all around me, searching for someone to fend it
> off. But I was told inside myself that there was no one. It gave
> me a feeling of terrible aloneness. . . . I stood on a soundless
> island in a tideless sea. . . .
>
> I consider that my real childhood ended with the com-
> ing of the pronouncements. True, I played, fought, and stud-
> ied with other children, but always I stood apart within. . . .
> Why? Why? A cosmic loneliness was my shadow. Nothing and
> nobody around me really touched me. It is one of the blessings
> of this world that few people see visions and dream dreams.

Hurston made of herself a repository of African American folk
and spiritual life, much of which would have disappeared except
that she recorded it and wrote it down and there it is, a diamond in
the stacks of thousands of libraries, while she spent the last years of

her rich life working at odd jobs, living on welfare, and ended her days supported by others and was buried with funds contributed by friends. Indeed, the life of a solitary can be a hard life to lead, and yet, after reading her memoir, her novels, and her anthropological writing, when I bring her to mind she is always wreathed in laughter.

Like so many great African American artists, musicians, and writers, Hurston was formed in the crucible of the church. An early intense and immersive experience of spirituality makes fertile soil for solitaries; one encounters at religious services stories of earlier solitaries as role models, with Jesus or the Buddha coming immediately to mind. The Bible, both Hebrew and Christian, is filled with stories of men and women acting out their destinies alone. Judith, Esther, even the much-maligned Eve—all are women who took their destinies in their own hands. The Virgin Mary, though in possession of an arranged husband, appears alone in the New Testament, in her apparitions (Guadalupe, Lourdes), and in folk mythology. A seventeen-hundred-year-old church—arguably the largest and most enduring of human institutions—that professes its dedication to the family—at least as defined during and since the Industrial Revolution—most often chooses solitaries to canonize as saints.

Hurston was poor in material belongings but not, by her own testimony, poor in spirit. This woman worked for every dollar that put food on her plate or kept a roof over her head—including most especially those dollars she was given by her white, wealthy benefactor, Charlotte Mason, who insisted that Hurston call her "Godmother."

Like all of Godmother's beneficiaries—like the poet and fellow solitary Langston Hughes, Hurston's confidant and friend—Hurston expended great quantities of psychic energy in flattering Mason, soothing her feathers when they were ruffled, and scraping and bowing when Godmother required it, which was often. How often must the accomplished, self-created Hurston have had to close her eyes and think of Florida! She was independent as a hog on ice, this woman who describes herself as having "a face looking like it had been chopped out of a knot of pine wood with a hatchet on somebody's off day." And yet accomplishing her goals required money, even for someone as skilled at living off the land as Hurston, and Godmother, with all her Anglo presumption, privilege, and arrogance, was its source.

Many readers know Hurston from her fine novel *Their Eyes Were Watching God*, but her lasting historical impact may rest equally in her detailed reporting of the sayings, stories, and practices of the transplanted African communities of the American South, the Caribbean, and Central America. In the 1920s, through an improbable concatenation of character, hard work, coincidence, luck, intelligence, dissemblance, and astute gambles, she found herself, a penniless orphan raised in Eatonville—one of the nation's first intentional black communities, located in central Florida—enrolled at Columbia University, where she came under the tutelage of Franz Boas, the "father of anthropology." Boas, who sent forth some of the great ethnographers—among them Margaret Mead—recognized in Hurston a woman whose background, spirit, and native curiosity would enable her to bear witness to customs and practices that African Americans wisely concealed, not only from white people, but sometimes from those of their own race. As a black woman and a Floridian, Hurston had unique access to Caribbean people and cultures.

Under Boas's sponsorship and with the on-again, off-again support of Godmother, Hurston infiltrated first the storytelling communities of Florida and then the voodoo cults of New Orleans and Haiti.

Every page of her books makes clear that Hurston's greatest love was for the story—a love so great that more than once she risked her life in its pursuit; a love so great that she saw facts as serviceable means to its end, but not the end in themselves. As a result, her reporting came under criticism from those (mostly Anglo) academics who fault her for getting involved with her subjects and for her willingness to stretch and mold fact in service to truth. But for Hurston to have approached her people as a dedicated empiricist—a way of being emphatically counter to their own practices and philosophies—would have sucked the life from their stories, the very life that Boas sent her out to chronicle. It would also have interfered with her singular capacity to earn their trust.

A mystic since childhood, Hurston responded so sympathetically to her investigations of voodoo that she eventually became an adept, apprenticing herself to more than one priest and learning its rituals and philosophy. "Voodoo is a religion of creation and life," she writes. "It is the worship of the sun, the water, and other natural forces, but the symbolism is no better understood than that of other religions and consequently is taken too literally." Eventually she was elevated to the rank of *hounci*, "a first-level initiate to the religion," according to her biographer Valerie Boyd, which title bound her to a code of secrecy that later hampered her ability to write forthrightly about her experiences.

She was criticized for her literal representation of dialect; in particular Richard Wright, the leading African American writer of the time, felt that she was catering to a white preconception of how "quaint" black people talked. In fact, as an anthropologist she was phonetically representing what she heard, with no ambitions or intentions of scrubbing the language so as to satisfy the demands of advocates of high Anglo diction. In any case, Hurston's accounts provide a record, in many cases our only sympathetic record, of Deep South and Caribbean communities now largely vanished. In this, too, she was ahead of her time: her sympathies are always on her sleeve and she makes no effort to hide them, an approach to anthropological recording and study that many of today's scholars credit as more honest and useful than pretending to a pseudo-scientific objectivity.

Like James Baldwin, like so many of our greatest African American writers and artists, she was a preacher's child, and over time she took the voodoo philosophy as hers and melded it with her father's African American Christianity into her own private religion. The men of her novels become preachers, even as the women, even those who have received the call, are denied. Hurston, who might well have herself become a powerful preacher, took writing as her pulpit, setting forth her spiritual philosophy in her memoir in a chapter entitled "Religion."

> . . . I do not pretend to read God's mind. If He has a plan of the Universe worked out to the smallest detail, it would be folly for me to presume to get down on my knees and attempt to revise it. That, to me, seems the highest form of sacrilege. So I do not pray. . . . The stuff of my being is matter, ever changing, ever moving, but never lost; so what need of denominations and creeds to deny myself the comfort of all my fellow men? . . . I am one with the infinite and need no other assistance.

In describing her beliefs, Hurston has made a prose poem from the philosophy of the seventeenth-century philosopher Baruch Spinoza, whom she read and admired, and it is no coincidence that these two advocates of discipline and individual responsibility were both solitaries and outcasts. In his home city of Amsterdam, Spinoza achieved the remarkable feat of being anathematized and exiled by both Jews and Christians, for (among other heresies) his suggestion that the Biblical stories were not literally true.

"I do not choose to admit weakness," Hurston writes, an interesting formulation, emphasizing as it does the walling out of weakness as an act of will. She lived as a secular monk, an adept of the religion of the self—Whitman's religion of love of self, Zweig's heresy of self-love—which, properly understood, is the very opposite of selfishness. Hurston's unique gift was to learn and understand both traditions, Christianity and voodoo, as different manifestations of the one great love force. She understood that institutions exist for men who construct and guard and embellish their power but that religion is an elemental urge which accommodates institutions where it must but which arises and flows with the force and inevitability of rivers. Roofs and walls she perceived as oppressive. She tells of a Haitian Catholic priest who tried to intimidate pilgrims by posting a policeman at the waterfall that was the destination of their annual sacred journey. "I fail to see," Hurston writes, "where it would have been more uplifting for them to have been inside a church listening to a man urging them to 'contemplate the sufferings of our Lord,' which is just another way of punishing one's self for nothing. It is very much better for them to climb the rocks in their bare clean feet and meet Him face to face in their search for the eternal in beauty."

"The search for the eternal in beauty"—that could be the mantra of each of the solitaries who have drawn me to themselves. Why give time and energy to the search for the eternal? Because our lives are at once both impermanent and enduring. The impermanence is easy; our society emphasizes it; we each know that we will die, the great democracy of death. But I have stumbled on a truth I would prefer to ignore: everything is always—including the poisonous chemicals used in manufacturing my cell phone, including me. Might I care for the earth better if I understood, really grasped, the truth that in their different ways mystics and scientists each tell us, that our every choice reverberates into the lives of those who follow, that there is no death, there is only life becoming more life?

Boyd, Hurston's biographer, points out that *Their Eyes Were Watching God* "is ultimately about self-love, about Janie's hard-willed choice to love nobody—not even the love of her life—more than she does herself." "I belong to no race nor time," Hurston wrote of herself, with characteristic panache. "I am the eternal feminine with a string of pearls." Hurston expressed her love of self not through accumulating money and power but through her love of her community and her love of her work. Faced with the challenge of making a life as a black professional woman from a working-class background at any time and place, but most especially under Jim Crow, she never compromised her commitment to writing, to storytelling, to art.

Hurston lived by her wits, which is to say by faith—faith in herself, faith in the integrity of her journey. Did her faith fail her at the end, when she moved from one tiny rental to another, one step ahead of landlords seeking payment? Or is this death reserved for the greatest of souls, those who go to their destinies owning nothing more than their shrouds?

Hurston married three times, once for four years during which she spent more time apart from her husband and pursuing divorce than she spent with him, and twice more for brief periods. Of "P.M.P.," the man she describes as "the real love of my life," she writes, "I really wanted to conform, but it was impossible." "I really wanted to do anything he wanted me to do, but that one thing I could not do," she writes. "It was not just my contract with my publishers, it was that I had things clawing inside of me that must be said . . . no matter how soaked we were in ecstasy, the telephone or the doorbell would ring and there would be my career again. A charge had been laid upon me and I must follow the call."

What a disservice to civilization, to impose on this free spirit, this great writer and servant to humanity, this great solitary, vows of either celibacy or marriage. "You are destroying yourself," cries Wing Biddlebaum to the young writer in the solitary Sherwood Anderson's classic short story "Hands." "You have the inclination to be alone and to dream and you are afraid of dreams. You want to be like others in town here. You hear them talk and you try to imitate them." *I really wanted to conform, but it was impossible. A charge had been laid upon me.* Again and again, solitaries invoke the passive voice in describing their relationship to their work and their choices. They understand that the solitary has been singled out (so to speak) by a force larger than himself or herself; that their calling is greater than the call to conformity, the call to convention, the call to marriage; that somehow, even in suffering, especially in suffering, the solitary is the special child of destiny.

Every one of us seeks to escape his mortal solitude, many of us so badly that we hitch up and tie down. So eager are we to give ourselves—so strong is the human impulse to generosity—that we are willing to hand over our particular selves to an architecture of emotion, a house of drama, the enduring three-legged sack race called marriage, even when we are clearly unsuited for the cause, even when repeated and bitter experience teaches us, or should teach us, that solitude is our proper calling. Of Hurston's novels, Boyd writes, "Marriage, Hurston seems to say, is a deadly proposition: someone has to give up his or her life." "I have a strong suspicion," Hurston writes, "but I can't be sure that much of what passes for constant love is a golded-up moment walking in its sleep."

   She knew the longing for union as well as or better than any of us; she wrote it out. "Oh, how I cried out to be just as everyone else!" But she understood her solitude as a calling, a destiny. "Even as I hoped I knew that the cup meant for my lips would not pass. I must drink the bitter drink." "Bitter," the most sensitive of the taste sensations, developed, some speculate, to enable us to perceive and avoid poisons—but, as every master chef knows, the most challenging and most interesting flavor to incorporate.

CHAPTER 10

A Man Alone, A Single Woman

Rod McKuen and Nina Simone

LISTENING TO THE LEGENDARY vocalist and civil rights activist Nina Simone, I find myself conceiving a new definition of a solitary—someone who is whole and complete unto herself, who cannot be complemented or completed by another because, like the voice that speaks to Moses from the burning bush, she is what she is. She has achieved what the Buddhists call "no duality"—no separation between interior and exterior, no scrim between the heart and the world.

Maybe that is what defines my solitaries: an intense consciousness of self, born of an intense sensual experience, born in turn of an indifference to developing or inability to develop a protective shell—a border wall between interior and exterior, between the world of the heart and the world of the mind, between self and other. "Anything musical made me quiver ecstatically," Simone wrote, "as if my body were a violin and somebody was drawing a bow across it."

This does not make for an easy path in society, where the most essential skill may be the art of the blank countenance—the exterior appearance concealing the interior life. Learning that Simone entitled her final album, issued in 1993, *A Single Woman,* I ordered the CD. What Simone's aged voice has lost in purity and range it has gained in poignance, and her singing contains the heartbreak and wisdom learned through her struggle to lead a successful musical career and stable emotional life in spite of the racism and hostility that she confronted at every step and that contributed to her battle with mental illness. "I live alone / That hasn't always been easy to do," she sings on the title cut, and later, "caught in a world few people understand."

Touched by the tender, world-weary words, I went in search of the lyricist, who turns out to have been her near contemporary Rod McKuen, the poet and composer whom critics loved to trash in the 1960s and 1970s. "The King of Kitsch," *Newsweek* called him. "Tailor-made for the 1960s," wrote a critic. "Poetry with a verse that drawled in country cadences from one shapeless line to the next, carrying the rusticated innocence of a Carl Sandburg thickened by the treacle of a man who preferred to prettify the world before he described it."

I wonder what the critic's phrase "prettify the world" would have meant to McKuen, born in an Oakland Salvation Army hostel, abandoned by his father at birth, physically and sexually abused by relatives, a high school dropout and street kid living by his wits and hand-to-mouth for most of his teens and early twenties before using the folk music scene to leverage himself, one poem or composition at a time, to international stardom. Though today he is largely forgotten, in 1969 he was a major force in the West Coast entertainment world, paid the ultimate compliment by Frank Sinatra, who recorded *A Man Alone: The Words and Music of McKuen,* including, among others, a song called "The Single Man" and the title cut "A Man

Alone," which includes the line—a sentiment Zora Neale Hurston also expresses—"A man who knows love is seldom what it seems / Only other people's dreams."

These albums, Simone's and Sinatra's with lyrics by McKuen, were musical collaborations among solitaries who recognized themselves as such and set out to give voice, literally, to their solitude. McKuen, a gay man, was the link between Simone and Sinatra—a lyricist who writes of and from the perspectives of both genders, the solitary man's and the solitary woman's. Is that because McKuen occupied an androgynous space in between? Does the similarity of the lyrics he composed for these two wildly different vocalists indicate lack of creativity on his part or an indication that the experience of solitude transcends gender?

The point is not that McKuen was laughing all the way to the bank, though he was, nor that his books sold millions of copies, though they did, nor that his lyrics were recorded by many of the great voices and musical artists of the twentieth century, though that is true, too, nor that he received a Grammy as well as two Academy Award nominations and a Pulitzer nomination for scores that he wrote for, among other films, *The Prime of Miss Jean Brodie,* or that he was the first artist to successfully demand integration of his concerts in South Africa, or that he introduced Belgian singer Jacques Brel to American audiences. The point is that he was a solitary—a self-defined solitary—an outsider, like Nina Simone, both playing and succeeding by their own rules, despite the racism (Simone) and homophobia (McKuen) they faced.

Asked to define himself, McKuen responded, quite sensibly, "Collectively I spend more hours brushing my teeth than having sex, so I refuse to define my life in sexual terms." The painter Edward Habib, sometimes identified as Edward Habib McKuen, lived with him; McKuen described him sometimes as his partner, sometimes as his brother. Various sources identify McKuen as having one or two children, though other sources don't mention children at all. His confused biography is a testimony to the man as a solitary—born, after all, with nothing to lose—who accepted no labels of any kind, though he called himself a "die-hard feminist." The titles of his books form a continuous lyric to solitude, among them *The Sound of Solitude,* where in a poem called "The Great Adventure" he writes, "Who can sing of solitude enough? / Why do we fear the word / as we do plague?"

So many of McKuen's songs, so much of his work, focuses on solitaries (e.g., the score for *The Prime of Miss Jean Brodie,* a film about a solitary) that I think of him as a poet and composer ahead of his time. From "Every Loner Has To Go Alone," sung as a duet with, to name only one of his prominent partners, Dolly Parton: "I've been alone a lifetime and I know / Every loner has to go alone." From "The Loner," sung by McKuen himself: "When I held my hand out / People turned their backs on me." He was a classic solitary, ever and always giving of himself. Throughout his career he worked for LGBT rights and hosted benefits for AIDS research and other LGBT-related causes. Later in life he published a memoir about the search for his biological father and donated the royalties to support the efforts of adopted children to locate their biological parents.

If the savage criticism bothered McKuen, that didn't reveal itself in his work; in 1977 he released an album capitalizing on the disco craze called *Slide . . . In Easy.* The European cover featured a muscular arm and hand digging a lump of vegetable shortening from a Crisco can relabeled "Disco." (I can't make this stuff up. Go find the image online.) It was the height of the gay revolution of the 1970s, and McKuen was thumbing his nose—or flipping his middle finger—at the button-down establishment so critical of his poetry, many of whom he might have encountered on a Saturday night in the don't-ask-don't-tell world of the gay bathhouses.

Is McKuen's poetry any good? The disco album is, in a word, terrible, even with generous allowance made for disco as a pop phenomenon. For sure he was a better lyricist than poet. The living presence of the performer and the backdrop of the score enables lyrics that on the page seem trite to achieve their full and intended effect. Read on the page, Tennessee Williams's plays seem melodramatic; delivered on the stage or in front of a camera by, say, the solitaries Vivien Leigh or Marlon Brando, they're searing. Rabindranath Tagore faced an analogous challenge. Responding to British critics who found his lyrics overwrought, Tagore wrote that reading his lyrics unaccompanied by their musical scores—the most common way they are encountered in the West—was comparable to encountering "butterflies without their wings." Accompanied by their melodies, the lyrics are less dated, more moving.

At the same time, it must be said: between Jacques Brel's "Ne Me Quitte Pas" and McKuen's English adaptation "If You Go Away," Simone chose to record the former, in a version that is the very embodiment and expression of heartbreak. That the French *sounds* more affecting is to be expected—that's inherent in the Romance roots of the language. But Brel's lyrics are better, with an ear for metaphor that McKuen can only imitate, not match; and Brel wrote the haunting score, which McKuen, though himself a composer, evidently knew better than to try to improve upon.

Like Nina Simone, like many solitaries, McKuen struggled with depression. Though a predilection to depression is surely genetic,

I assume that with both Simone and McKuen, their experience of depression incorporated the burdens of fame combined with the constant assaults on their integrity—Simone because of her race, McKuen because of his sexuality, both because of their solitude. To my ear, the viciousness of the critical assessments frequently directed at each of them suggests, not measured critical judgment, but bullying. What I take away—what I hold in my heart—is the vision of these deeply wounded solitaries, Simone and McKuen, transforming suffering into art.

Recognized by her small North Carolina community as a prodigy, Simone began her career as a classical musician and vocalist. When she was denied a career in classical music because, she believed, of her race, she changed her name and began singing jazz in suburban bars and clubs. Throughout her career she longed to be taken seriously by the classical music world, in the way that McKuen longed to be embraced as a legitimate poet. But critics build reputations by defining and enforcing distinctions between "high" and "low," "worthy" and "pop" art. Tagore and, later, Bob Dylan were able to transcend categories, but Tagore had a family fortune and his country's support, and Dylan was white and straight. Simone and McKuen were fighting the invisible, powerful forces of racism and homophobia, with exclusion from the realm of "high art" a potent weapon in their critics' arsenal of oppression.

Fearless, Simone was unified in herself; she was unwilling, indeed unable, to accommodate injustice on or off stage—but that inability or indifference to bending and shaping one's self to others' sensibilities comes at a price. The woman who wrote and sang "Mississippi Goddam" and on the same album so movingly renders "Black Is The Color Of My True Love's Hair" was not two different vocalists, however radically different the songs are in tone and message. Rather, Simone was capable of expressing a symphony's range of emotion, from fury to love, with all the blends and stops between.

Interviewed in *What Happened, Miss Simone?*, the documentary about Simone's life, speaking of her writing and singing "Mississippi Goddam," comedian Dick Gregory said, "We were all thinking [of those lyrics]—but *she wrote them*," thumping his leg for emphasis.

Indeed Simone wrote those lyrics, and sang them, and took the heat—but the heat, day after day, takes its cumulative toll. If Simone sometimes saw bogeymen where none existed, maybe that was because she had been blindsided enough times by real bogeymen which she had not anticipated. In her largely dictated autobiography *I Put a Spell on You*, Simone tells how isolated she was by her talent—and by the burden of carrying her mother's hopes that she would be a standard-bearer for her race. "Momma . . . had a special gift when it came to letting the family know what she wanted. Without anyone being aware of her saying anything specific, her wishes became known"—in this case, the insistence that her daughter would be the world's first successful black woman concert pianist.

Even during her years of professional instruction, Simone charted her own course. "My future was as much in my own hands as those of my teachers," she says in her autobiography. "They pointed me in various musical directions, but I was doing the exploring on my own"—another self-taught solitary. And yet her talent and her music came accompanied by demons as well as angels. Sometimes she writes of the joy she found in playing, but always the music came accompanied by solitude. "How lonely the music made me," she told her ghostwriter. "I was regarded as an exception, not like [my classmates]. I was out on my own"—and it is "the thing that makes you exceptional," wrote her close friend and, some say, lover, the playwright Lorraine Hansberry, "that also makes you lonely." Was Simone denied admission to Philadelphia's Curtis School of Music because of her race? "The wonderful thing about this type of discrimination is that you can never know for sure if it is true, because no one is going to turn around and admit to being a racist," Simone said. "At the same time there's the nagging worry that maybe that isn't it at all, maybe it's just because you're just no good."

In the end, as is so often the case in the careers of dedicated artists and solitaries, rejection caused her to work harder. Her project became the transposition and integration of classical technique and complexity of composition and phrasing onto and into the modern vernaculars of folk, blues, and jazz. She is thus among the pioneers in crafting the marvelous crazy quilt of international influences and techniques that constitutes contemporary music; but she never entirely gave up that original goal, the goal of her mother and her teachers, that she would become the first great black classical pianist. "The direction of my life was determined by other ambitions and their money and I was promised a future I had no part in choosing," she said in her autobiography, echoing the situation of so many other writers and artists from lower economic classes. "In return for this great act of faith by everyone I ever knew I applied myself with dedication and turned my back on everything but the fulfillment of *our* [my emphasis] destiny." "Our" may mean members of her family, of course, and the donors to the fund set up to further her education. But she dictated her autobiography late in her life, by which point "our" had presumably come to mean her people—African and African American people.

Simone makes clear that she feels as if, like Zora Neale Hurston, she sacrificed her personal life to her career, and no doubt the demands on a talented black woman were such that only a rare individual would be able to make a whole life from these competing strands. And yet, in the end, like Hurston but with less self-awareness, she emerges as a solitary—someone so complete and rounded in herself that she allowed no room for a partner, even as she devoted time and energy to finding one. As she tacitly acknowledges in her autobiography, Simone needed less a spouse than a business manager, a role that, as she repeatedly acknowledges, her husband Andy Stroud filled. He also slapped her around and at least once beat her savagely, an instance of domestic violence that he later acknowledged and excused as a justified response to what he saw as her flirting and "fooling around with guys and girls."

"I married him because I needed desperately to love somebody," Simone said, epitomizing in a sentence the solitary's challenge: what to do with, where to direct the passion that resides in our hearts, which seeks to love one at the same time as loving all. The book version of *What Happened, Miss Simone?* quotes an especially disturbing letter from Simone to Stroud: "not the beatings, Andy, not the beatings—those I can't take—for some reason, they destroy everything in me—my confidence, my warmth, and my spirit! . . . I do understand and I respect the message you so crudely got across (smile) that message was 'I will be heard I will be seen I will love you And you will love me back, or I'll kill you!!!!'"

I think back to Eudora Welty's traveling salesman's plea: "[My heart] should be flooded with love. . . . Come and stand in my heart, whoever you are, and a whole river would cover your feet and rise higher and take your knees in whirlpools, and draw you down to itself, your whole body, your heart too." And then I think of the evolution Welty and Dickinson made, from longing for a partner to an embrace of solitude as a gift and destiny. For a host of reasons—the hard life of the performer, racism, sexism, her fragile, artistic sensibility, and more—Simone seems never to have reached that inner peace. All her life she preserved as an ideal her unconsummated relationship when she was seventeen with a young Cherokee man who was, according to her, as much in love with her as she with him. But given her already-demonstrated commitment to her art, had they married, the marriage might well have been stormy and short-lived. Had Simone accepted her solitude—or, alternatively, had she lived in a society that accepted and celebrated solitaries, especially solitary artists, especially solitary black women artists—she would surely have had an easier path.

What happened, indeed, in those years? "People came to see me because they knew I was singing close to the edge and one day I might fail," Simone says, and her comment contains the troubling fact that audiences and readers are as, maybe more, eager to see an artist fail than to see her succeed. Everyone slows to gawk at the roadside wreck. For audio evidence, search out and compare Lotte Lenya's performance of her husband Kurt Weill's song "Pirate Jenny" from his play (co-created with Bertolt Brecht) *The Threepenny Opera,* and compare it to Nina Simone's performance of the same song. Lenya is polished and competent, but Simone finds and mines the heart of the lyrics, summing up in one song a rage and heartbreak and, yes, hatred born of millennia of oppression. Lenya is acting a role; Simone is living it. Simone teaches us how and why the poor of eighteenth-century Paris so eagerly embraced the guillotine.

"How could royalty stomp around in the mud and still walk with grace?" asks Dr. Betty Shabazz, widow of Malcolm X, in the documentary *What Happened, Miss Simone?* "Most people are afraid to be as honest as she lived." To cultivate and express that range of heart, Simone paid the highest price—that of her sanity, and finally, her art. Her listeners were and are her beneficiaries—if only we would act to change the world, as she would have us do, rather than play her CDs for the frisson of being in the presence of royalty and then go about our lives unchanged.

"Queen Nina" was finally diagnosed with bipolar syndrome and placed on medication, which calmed her but slurred her voice and interfered with her piano technique. But how might a solitary, unified heart encompass both the adulation of the audiences who came to hear her sing and the attack dogs and fire hoses and tear gas the white police used against her people? Who is sick in this story, Simone or her society? Her struggle brings to mind Emily Dickinson:

> Much Madness is divinest Sense—
> To a discerning Eye—
> Much Sense—the starkest Madness—
> 'Tis the Majority
> In this, as All, prevail—
> Assent—and you are sane—
> Demur—you're straightway dangerous—
> And handled with a Chain—

> [#435]

How could Simone continue to perform, night after night, knowing that her anguish and grief and suffering and anger were our entertainment? Her illness was a symptom; white America was, if not the cause, at least a complicating factor. Through some astonishing psychological strength and sleight of hand, James Baldwin was able to turn the hatred and prejudice into fuel—though, like Simone, he lived and died in another country. "I ask the white man: Why do you need a nigger?" Baldwin wrote. "What is it in you that needs a nigger?" Somewhere, somehow, he found the strength to live with that question, but Simone broke under the strain.

Simone's civil rights work—her revolutionary work ("Mississippi Goddam," indeed) underscores her plaintive comment: "I could finally answer Momma's great unasked question, 'Why do you sing out in the world when you could be praising God?'" The shooting of Medgar Evers, then the deaths of four girls in the Birmingham bombing and, later, two protesters enabled her to see what her black audiences had already perceived: in her writing and performing she *was* praising her God. "Whatever it was that happened out there under the lights," she says, "it mostly came from God, and I was just a place on the line He was moving on." "Those kids out in the backwoods knew I was part of their fight before I knew it myself," she said, "and when I finally met up with them, the 'stormtroopers of the movement' . . . who risked their lives every day . . . I had no choice but to line up alongside them. You can call it what you like, but for me it seemed like destiny."

In *I Put a Spell on You,* Simone describes the relationship between her music and her encounter with and understanding of God.

How do you explain what it feels like to get on the stage and make poetry that you know sinks into the hearts and souls of people who are unable to express it? How do you talk about that? There aren't many words, but in some way you know that tonight is a good thing. That's God.

I am very aware that I am an instrument. I have fights with God every day. . . . I've been given the gift of being able to play by ear, having perfect pitch . . . When you have this gift, you must give it back to the world. . . . I don't know if I can explain any better than that what God is.

Here, as in so many ways, Simone sets an example: she takes the word "God" and remakes it in the light of her experience. Like Hurston, she redefines God in the light of her own vision and understanding.

Simone wrote and spoke often of her close friendship with Lorraine Hansberry, author of *A Raisin in the Sun*, the first play by an African American woman to be performed on Broadway. Hansberry played a critical role in raising Simone's political consciousness. "[Lorraine Hansberry and I] never talked about men or clothes or other such inconsequential things," Simone said in her autobiography. ". . . It was always Marx, Lenin, and revolution—real girls' talk." When Hansberry, only thirty-four years old, lay dying in the hospital, Simone went to her room with a record player. "I played 'In The Evening By The Moonlight' for her . . . the next time I played 'In The Evening By The Moonlight' was at her funeral service."

Reading of Simone choosing "In The Evening By The Moonlight" to play at Lorraine Hansberry's deathbed and memorial service, I went again in search of the lyricist—why did Simone choose that old chestnut for this tender parting moment—to discover that many of these classics of the vaudeville era came, as Simone surely knew but I did not, from the pen of Jimmy Bland, born in 1854, a self-taught African American and solitary who, like Zora Neale Hurston, rose to the heights of society and international fame only to die poor and obscure, buried in an unmarked grave.

Only now, in studying Bland's lyrics, do I find the references to slavery. The traditionally rollicking chorus of "In The Evening By The Moonlight" is preceded by a slow-paced stanza:

In the evening by the moonlight
When my mother had finished working
We used to sit around the fire place
Till the cornbread it was done . . .
It's the only time they ever gave us to spare
To have a little fun

In her 1960 recording of the song, Simone pauses meaningfully after the lines, "It's the only time they ever gave us to spare / to have a little fun"—then chuckles, then continues into the cheerful up-tempo shift of the original, customary orchestration. Singing the same song thirty years later, Simone, visibly ravaged by mental and emotional illness, is an angry, broken woman performing because she needs the money and because it's what she does. She interrupts the song to issue a blunt command to the drummer—"Don't speed it up"—thereby eliminating the gay up-tempo shift in favor of preserving the melancholy tone of the opening stanza, with its reference to slavery, even into its chorus.

The tune and some—not all—of the lyrics to "In The Evening By The Moonlight" are buried deep in my DNA because these were the songs my parents and their friends sang far into the night on the flagstone patio. The home my father built featured not one but two flagstone patios, built with stone pulled from neighboring creeks. The flagstones were of pleasingly varied shapes, a result of being harvested by hand, one by one, on summer afternoons when the family went to the creek. Though Father daily walked across the U.S. highway to his job at the distillery, I recall no clear distinction in my parents' lives between work and play. Mother watched the little ones splashing in the water while Father went looking for flat stones to pry loose from the creekbed and, with the help of the older brothers, to harvest. These they assembled into a jigsaw mosaic patio that, so far as I could tell, involved no stone cutting but was nonetheless straight-edged on all sides.

How I wish I could have hovered overhead to watch as they assembled it! Certain rocks were shaped like states: Minnesota, for sure; a great hunk that was a reasonable facsimile of the southern half of Texas, including the sinuous Rio Grande border; Vermont. These were limestone of the Mississippian Era, some three hundred-plus million years old, pocked with crinoids and cephalopods and brachiopods and trilobites.

From mid-spring to late autumn, the flagstone patio was the gathering spot of choice. My memory preserves it as a single ongoing party, where the spirits of a family and community pass through and overlay each other, each moment creating pentimenti for the next, until the space is become dense with images and sound, as if a photographic plate had been continuously exposed at the same time that an audiotape had been continuously recording . . . all the moments and all the conversations are simultaneously distinct and blended.

In what manner, please, are those people absent and gone, when they make up the very stuff of me and now you, in the miraculous way of words in print? Gerald and Margaret Barry, those genial alcoholics, with Gerald picking out tunes on his ukelele. He had the thespian blood of the Irish, I now understand, as well as their genetic predisposition to dipsomania. The monks sitting in the Adirondack chairs my father built, my mother ever their center of attention—she always ready for an audience and always ready to stretch a meal with a can of soup or a batch of biscuits to feed whoever showed up on the doorstep; ever and always welcoming the stranger, the traveler, the bringer of news from the great outside world into our big-family, small-town life.

The roster of songs was largely unvarying—Mr. Barry was not into learning new tunes—but certain favorites signaled the party's winding down: "In The Evening By The Moonlight," "Darktown Strutters' Ball," "Oh, Dem Golden Slippers," and, finally and inevitably, "Goodnight, Irene." In singing "In The Evening By The Moonlight," my parents and their friends never sang—probably had never heard—the verse referencing slavery; for them, the song transitioned directly from the "old folks singing" and "banjos ringing" to the perennially upbeat chorus.

That song, those voices, my mother in the lead, directing with her famously pointed index finger, echo in my imagination. With

Simone and Jimmy Bland, the singers are all dead, but in my heart I hear them on the flagstone patio, singing late into in the evening, by the moonlight . . . more evidence of Whitman's claim that there is no death, and that for all his troubles and woes, Jimmy Bland, through Nina Simone and my mother and in my heart, still lives.

CHAPTER 11

Those Who Seek Beauty Will Find It

Bill Cunningham

NEW YORK AND SAN FRANCISCO—both ports of entry for immigrants—are arguably the most civilized cities in the U.S. because from the first they were cities of and for solitaries. The creative imagination, liberated by immigration, freed from constraints of church and family, grounded in but not oppressed by tradition, made both cities trend-setters. These are cities built on and for desire: desire for sex and money and power, of course, but, most importantly, and always present as the bass line of those desires, desire for beauty—a force so powerful that it would lead someone to abandon a life that, whatever its trials, was at least familiar, and set out as a seeker.

Which brings me to Bill Cunningham, a votary of beauty whose passion happened to be hats.

Cunningham was made famous beyond the world of fashion photography by *Bill Cunningham: New York,* a documentary love letter to each of its subjects, and by "On the Street," his weekly column for the *New York Times* "Style" section, which he published until shortly before his death in 2016. Cunningham, who through his photography became the fashion arbiter of the city, lived for most of his life alone, in a closet of an apartment (no kitchen, no private bathroom) atop Carnegie Hall. There he filed decades of his negatives in boxes and slept on a pallet laid on top of them. Though wealthy friends believed him to have been born to high society—in the documentary, one comments, "only someone born to wealth could live so simply," an observation that reveals a great deal about the privilege of the speaker—in fact he grew up in a traditional Boston middle-class family from whom he distanced himself when he dropped out of Harvard and took up making hats in confections as fanciful and outré as he was polite and well-mannered. In the 1960s, with hats having gone the way of the ivory-billed woodpecker exterminated for their sake, he took up fashion writing and then, as a logical segue, fashion photography.

That a man in Cunningham's position was able to sustain his earnestness and enthusiasm across a lifetime is a testimonial to the deepest imaginable faith. To call him a "fashion arbiter" understates his contribution, though in the documentary the editor of *Vogue* says, "We all dress for Bill." He sought not celebrity but beauty, the self-conscious effort to make a statement, to imitate the original act of creation, to write a verse in the great ongoing human drama.

The man was a saint, though not, for me, a role model. I love good food and drink—Cunningham was content with an Egg McMuffin; I love the conviviality of the table—at society dinners Cunningham would be behind his camera, working the crowd. And yet I readily claim him as a teacher. "Teach the gospel," St. Francis of Assisi advised, "and if you must, use words." Bill Cunningham did not use words. He was possessed of a radical openness, with the result that no small thing escaped his eye. In the documentary he projects the exuberance of a child, capering about with his arms flapping after blowing out in one breath all the candles on his eightieth birthday cake. He's not childish but wise—even if his camera functioned as a protective device for a gay man in a world where acknowledging himself as such would cost him his profession, since "don't ask, don't tell" prevailed even in the world of high fashion. One could be fey, one could be swish, but getting and keeping a job required submission to the rule of the closet, which dictated that everyone be publicly heterosexual.

Reading Cunningham's book, *Fashion Climbing: A Memoir with Photographs,* I am struck by the sense that life was more fun, in those days when the squares lived in the far-flung suburbs and abandoned the grubby inner cities to the creative and adventuresome. Among other tales, Cunningham describes costuming for an evening ball at the Waldorf-Astoria, when he clothed a woman friend in feathers and brought along two chickens to accessorize. He dusted the chickens with glitter and attached them to rhinestone leashes, but in the crush of the crowd the leashes broke. He spent the evening chasing the glittering chickens, one of which escaped out the door to Park Avenue. The second he caught and the next day slaughtered ("we had no money for food") for lunch.

He reveled in the glamor of those evenings, but between, in a pattern commonplace among my solitaries, he immersed himself in his work to the exclusion of society. "I didn't have many friends during those times . . . as the designing was so rewarding I didn't feel the need for people," he wrote. "I felt that people might influence me, and I wasn't going to take the chance."

His greatest gift lay in teaching us not how to dress, though there is that, but *how to see*—the gift of paying attention. His gift, evident in every photograph, is his love. "I eat with my eyes," he says, and the photographs seduce less by their audacity than through the joy apparent in every click of his shutter.

Oh, that spontaneous, infectious, all-embracing grin! Who could resist? "If you don't take money, they can't tell you what to do," he says—the man who tore up checks when his editors tried to pay him. "That's the key to the whole thing: don't take money." Evidently he took *some* money, but New York in those years was cheap, more so for those who had lived for decades in a rent-controlled room.

He implies that he has been a lifelong celibate (though one reason he goes to church is "to repent," he says with a grin). Even though he is wielding a camera, that potent modern-day weapon, he can photograph strangers because he is possessed of a good cheer that roots itself in his lack of sexual affect—although he is a solitary man, he emanates not threat or danger but professionalism leavened by delight, a single-pointed focus, pun intended, on the moment and the photograph.

The opening titles label him a "loner," but he's not a loner—he who loved nothing more than a good party; he's an outsider, a solitary, an eccentric, a secular monk. In my childhood vernacular we would have called him a *character*, a word that carried a hint of admiration and even envy for someone courageous enough to seek and live out her or his idiosyncratic destiny. Like Walt Whitman, he was a free spirit not enslaved to the mania of owning things. When Cunningham and the few remaining tenants were ejected from their Carnegie Hall apartments to make room for telemarketers and the city relocated Cunningham to a Central Park South apartment, he had the landlord remove the appliances to make room for his files. When he traveled to Paris to accept the decoration of Chevalier of the Legion of Honor, he wore his signature blue smock—designed for Parisian street sweepers—and, when it rained, his black plastic poncho patched with duct tape.

When the interviewer asks Cunningham if he's ever had a romantic relationship, Cunningham says immediately—as if he's been waiting for this question, though his interviewer has not implied it and seems nonplussed at his response—"Oh, you want to know about gay." After that, Cunningham's response is circuitous and convoluted, though to this point in the film he has been the model of openness and simplicity. "A relationship never occurred to me," he says—a statement characteristic of gay people of Cunningham's age. "It was all about the clothes." Asked if he regrets that, he considers for a moment, then responds no. "I didn't have time!" he says with a laugh, but the laugh is clearly a mask, a façade, as he shifts from the intimate "I" to the distancing and impersonal "you": "You do have bodily urges," he says. "You control them as best you can."

Next, the interviewer asks him about church—why he attends Roman Catholic mass every Sunday, what religion means to him. Cunningham opens his mouth to respond, and then his face crumples and he's so overcome with emotion that he looks at the floor, his shoulders trembling. The filmmaker says gently, "You don't have to answer that." But Cunningham regains self-control and says that church is important to him, that he "needs it," without elaborating why.

The moment becomes a koan for each viewer, onto which we project something of ourselves. Thus it is that art teaches us to recognize and inhabit truth as well as recognizing those who, under the guise of slogans and doctrines, set themselves against it. Cunningham has made a sacrifice of the first magnitude—the sacrifice of a particular love—for a grander and higher and more generous beauty, a sacrifice that is sacred and thus the proper domain of religion. And then he is rejected by the Roman church, which labels him "objectively disordered," whose all-male power elite is terrified of real saints, true saints who might show them up for what they are—bureaucrats who have made the most commonplace of bargains, exchanging virtue for power and status.

The contradiction is intensified because, as Cunningham notes in his interview, it was the Roman church that first taught him how to see—taught him the importance of theater and the clothing/vestments/costumes that accompany it, the nature of beauty and the importance of creating and finding and celebrating it. For Cunningham, the streets of New York are a secular version of sacred theater, and he is the very model of the solitary who chooses to give his love to every person rather than to one.

A few years back I was in a cab filled with writers when one reported that a superstar pop trio had publicly announced their commitment to celibacy. Snickers all around. "Is that really possible?" someone asked. "I mean, do you think it's possible for a healthy person to be celibate?" Debate on this question ensued. I, who hadn't been unclothed in the presence of another person in longer than memory, held my tongue.

These writers, all of whom were partnered and in their thirties or forties, agreed that a victim of an accident or of war or illness might have to make peace with a life without sex. Otherwise they were unanimous in questioning the legitimacy of the announcement. "It's a public relations ploy," someone announced, to nods of assent. A commitment to celibacy, my colleagues in writing decided, is either a gimmick or indicative of some deep-seated psychological trauma.

I know so many people who tell me they are celibate—many within marriage—that these writers' unwillingness to accept the practice strikes me as evidence of a failure of knowledge (how ignorant they must be of intellectual history, to be so unaware of the long list of celibate geniuses), a failure of imagination (how strange that as writers they presume their reality is of necessity everyone's reality), how thoroughly they have bought into the myth that life organizes itself around the literal fact of who puts what where how often, rather than the richer and more complex manifestations of desire.

Counter to the avalanche of messages from popular culture, I practice celibacy not as negation (I resign myself to a sexless life and take up needlepoint or muscle cars to dispel the energy) but as a joyous turning inward. "Inebriate of air, debauchee of dew"—this from Emily Dickinson, most promiscuous of celibates.

To couple is to seek the most natural of unities, the unity with another person expressed and embodied in the act of coitus, a word used to mean "meeting" or "unity" long before it came to be associated with sex. In the first millennium of the Christian church—before the Christian church institutionalized marriage as the foundation of its worldly power—coitus *defined* marriage: marriage took place in the bed, not in the church. The priest merely blessed a sacrament the couple had already acted out or would act out. Sex—specifically, penetration—was the sacrament, a word whose root translates as "sacred oath." In the early Christian church, marriage was not, to recall Charlotte Stant's response to her billionaire suitor, "the condition"; the church set about adopting it as such in the Middle Ages, as an important tool in its rise to secular power. Later, as the church lost its armies and lands, it set about enforcing its will by requiring belief in increasingly elaborate dogmas (e.g., papal infallibility, implemented simultaneously with the loss of the last Papal States) and by dictating the policies and practices of ostensibly secular governments, among them the bureaucratic certification of marriage as a requirement for its validity. But in those early centuries of Christianity, marriage was not about property but was a public acknowledgment of the holy nature of sex—one partner making herself or himself vulnerable to her or his mate.

"Who puts what where how often" is in fact important, not because of the obsessions of the homophobes and the misogynists but because in sex the receptive partner is vulnerable, open, at greater risk. These, it turns out, are the essential qualities of love, the essential qualities of queer. And so the contemporary definition of "queer," finally—under which rubric I would include most, maybe all, of my solitaries—is not what one does in bed but one's stance toward the *ancien régime*, the status quo, the dominant mode, the way things have always been done; a willingness to take risks, to be vulnerable and open, the same vulnerability that Bill Cunningham exudes. Thoreau elaborates:

> Be the . . . Lewis and Clark of your own streams and oceans;
> explore your own higher latitudes . . . be a Columbus to whole
> new worlds within you, opening new channels, not of trade,
> but of thought. . . . it is easier to sail many thousand miles
> through cold and storm and cannibals . . . than it is to explore
> the private sea; the Atlantic and Pacific Ocean of one's being
> alone. . . . Let them wander . . . I have more of God, they
> more of the road.

"I have more of God . . ." Yes, exactly so. That is the *super*natural unity; that is the interior journey's goalless goal, the solitary's reward.

Solitude and celibacy are related but not necessary conditions. I have known party-hopping celibates; I have known promiscuous solitaries. But a conscious decision to refrain from sex can be a powerful incarnation of solitude. Actively inhabited celibacy represents a decision to commit oneself for whatever length of time to a discipline—to forgo one delight (the charms of dalliance, the pleasures of light company) for a different, longer-term undertaking, the deepening of the self.

My monk friends, men and women, brothers and sisters, speak with passion of celibacy as a conscious decision to fulfill oneself through love of many rather than of one—a communion with all rather than with a particular individual. "Instead of limiting myself to one person," they say, "I decided to open myself to everyone and, through everyone, to God." To my ears, a generous and lovely assertion. But I add wryly that in the 1970s, gay friends who hung out in San Francisco's bathhouses described their promiscuous nights in nearly identical terms: *I choose to give myself to everybody instead of to just one person.* More than one added, *And that's my religion.*

The echo is not coincidental. Celibacy and libertinism are antipodes, opposing poles that define desire. They are more similar than different, and each is populated by people of great desire. The key is to see one's solitude ever and always as an opportunity—a suffering, yes, but through that suffering a continual opening to the grandeur and possibilities of love; not what conservative *New York Times* columnist Ross Douthat called "deep familial selfishness," but Whitman's love of "cameradoes"—love of everyone, especially the outlier.

༄

In the 1930s my mother danced on tabletops and wore skirtless bathing suits and was seduced from teetotaling Protestantism into Roman Catholicism by the smells and bells, incense and music that she encountered in her one semester in college, where she roomed across the street from a Roman Catholic church. Marrying my father provided an excuse for a conversion to which she had long been drawn—the most rebellious and exotic, passionate act that a woman from the Bible Belt could accomplish.

I am grateful for a lifetime to the Roman church, because it instilled in me a sense of mystery and of manners (to invoke the solitary Flannery O'Connor's phrase), and to my mother for laying down a foundation of Protestant skepticism for that potent mix. She lies dying as I write these words, and in her honor I inject some leavening into my treatment of what should be a cheerful topic, by returning to Zora Neale Hurston, who wrote in *Dust Tracks on a Road:*

> Under the spell of moonlight, music, flowers, or the cut and smell of good tweeds, I sometimes feel the divine urge for an hour or day or maybe a week. Then it is gone and my interest returns to corn pone and mustard greens, or rubbing a paragraph with a soft cloth. Then my ex-sharer of a mood calls up in a fevered voice and reminds me of every silly thing I said, and eggs me on to say them all over again. It is the third presentation of turkey hash after Christmas. . . . I was sincere for the moment in which I said the things. It is strictly a matter of time. It was true for the moment, but the next day or the

next week, is not that moment. . . . So the great difficulty lies in trying to transpose last night's moment to the day which has no knowledge of it. That look, that tender touch, was issued by the mint of the richest of all kingdoms. That same expression today is utter counterfeit, or at best the wildest of inflation. What could be more zestless than passing out cancelled checks? It is wrong to be called faithless under circumstances like that. What to do?

I have met free spirits who so clearly express their untrammeled selves that their partners know from the first what they're getting into. I am not such a person, nor, do I think, are most of us. Most of us need limits; we thrive within limits. But I know that I, a gay man, am lucky to have been chosen for the demimonde, which taught me that love, true love, real love, divine love exists outside and apart from the laws of (mostly) men.

That my long bachelorhood may end tomorrow I do not doubt. Asked by a middle-aged woman when she would find love, my Zen teacher scratched his head and responded, "Maybe next Wednesday?" The most stable of marriages have been known to founder. Monks and priests have left their religious orders on a moment's notice, even as lifelong bachelors and spinsters couple and marry late in their lives.

But I have lived a long time alone. I seek to live not in anticipation but in embrace of the life I have been given. A great deal of virtue is born of necessity. I may not have chosen to be single in midlife, and I may not have chosen to be celibate, but here is me, I am it. I can choose simply to endure it with my attention focused elsewhere and outward. I can see my life without sex as a way-station, a year or a decade long, between sexual encounters. Or I can inhabit it, counter to all the messages of contemporary culture, as a legitimate way of being, an opportunity to focus all that longing on my heart's deepest desire, whether that be a community garden plot or teaching or world peace or writing a book.

The English Catholic G. K. Chesterton wrote, "Virtue is not the absence of vices or the avoidance of moral dangers; virtue is a vivid and separate thing, like pain or a particular smell. . . . Chastity does not mean abstention from sexual wrong; it means something flaming, like Joan of Arc." Chesterton was a monumental man, a ruddy-faced hippo of a man, who may have been sexually chaste but was famously promiscuous in his pursuit of other pleasures, notably booze. And I would expand his invocation of "chastity" to include moderation in all matters—including self-mortification, including alcohol. All the same, "something flaming"—desire not as a conflagration but as a steadily burning, light-giving lamp—strikes me as a fine description of what the celibate aspires to. Teresa of Avila and John of the Cross—or, for that matter, Jesus and the Buddha—did not take themselves *above* desire. They took charge of desire and so successfully focused it inward that they could then turn its energy outward. They sought not to raise themselves above the created world—the errand of a fool or a tyrant—but to more thoroughly integrate themselves into it.

In place of Chesterton's "chastity," I favor the Buddhist phrase "right conduct." A vow to practice right conduct strikes me as more flexible, more encompassing, and more challenging than a vow of celibacy. Such a vow places responsibility and the struggle where it belongs—with the individual conscience. Contained within celibacy, whether practiced or contemplated, is the asking of an essential question, more important now than ever; a question with radical implications for capitalism and for science as it is practiced under capitalism; a question of restraint: because I *can* do something, *must* I do it?

Celibacy is a discipline, a way of being, a stance toward one's fellow men and women—an agreement with the self to allow the dragon of desire a well-earned nap, while diverting its energies to other ends. In any case, after a certain point the dragon of desire wants to curl up in the corner by the fire, dozing in sweet recollection of past triumphs and, yes, even defeats, for now, long after the fact, they glow with the patina of memory.

Popular interpretations of Dickinson and James, Thoreau and Cunningham so often pity their long celibacies. But pity is a polite form of condescension; it is a way of measuring and thereby comprehending that which cannot be measured or understood; it is like Thomas Aquinas setting out to use reason to prove the existence of God. For infinity draws me onward, the earth draws me back to the stardust from which I am made. In my deepest heart I long to be one with the One; death along with birth is only a particularly striking milestone on a journey that, properly understood, has no beginning and no end. Time, as the quantum physicists tell us, is an illusion; and if time is an illusion, then death is an illusion. All moments are present to this moment—a truth that, like any good koan, cannot be explained but instead must be lived out.

♋

And yet how I miss the touch of a familiar and shaping hand; how I miss, not the sex but what precedes and follows it, the intimacy and the alienation, the strangeness to the other and to oneself, the being naked to another, the being naked to oneself. *Post coitum omne animal tristis est*—"after sex every animal is sad." I miss the sadness. And I miss even the arguments, because underlying the bickering was always this taken-for-granted fact: *how much I must matter to this person, that I rouse him to such anger!* How many relationships endure not from love but because one or both partners fear solitude more than they fear mayhem?

Staying with friends recently, a couple who met in their twenties but did not marry until their sixties, and then so as to protect each other's inheritance rights: After I retired, I heard them upstairs, preparing for bed, then woke in the night as one shifted in bed or snored. What a remarkable thing, I thought as I lay alone in the darkness, to know another's body over so many years! What great love they share! What comparable joys and sorrows can solitude offer?

I hear the answer in this quiet room; I see it in the angle of the autumn sun. The solitary forgoes openness to one for openness to all. Through all, I seek the One, the great Alone, a supernatural unity.

Like marriage for the coupled, the hard calling to solitude is a self-imposed discipline. The great, the incomparable reward of being alone is the opportunity, if I can be large enough to rise to its occasion, of encountering the great silence at the core of being, a silence that is at the same time uniquely mine and one with the background hum of the universe. To live for the changing of the light seems adequate reward.

I am not offering a rose-strewn path. The solitary's journey is fraught. Again and again our solitaries present us with this bedrock philosophy of previous ages, this truth so unpopular in our consumerist age: the path to liberation lies through suffering. The journey to peace lies not around but through suffering. Whitman in the hospitals, Dickinson in her room: the self is the vehicle, the boat that takes us from loneliness to aloneness—that takes us on the journey from loneliness to solitude.

From *Bill Cunningham: New York,* the image that persists is not of Cunningham in his blue street sweeper's smock among the swells, or even Cunningham choking up before the members of the French Academy of the Legion of Honor as he speaks of his lifelong search for beauty, but the eighty-year-old Cunningham donning his reflective vest and climbing onto his Schwinn, his twenty-ninth bicycle, to ride half the length of Manhattan in the dark, from Tribeca to the Upper West Side, to photograph a benefit. He who almost certainly never studied Buddhism summarizes it in a few phrases. "I don't decide anything," he says. "I let the street speak to me. You got to stay on the street and let the street tell you what it wants. There are no shortcuts." That nonjudgmental, all-embracing gaze can arise from the teachings of the Buddha and Jesus, or from the scientist's conscientious commitment to look at the world not as she wants it to be but as it is. That, it strikes me, is the foundation for real, honest, transformative love.

Creating and sustaining an intimate relationship is one way of making beauty, yes. For many reasons or no reasons Cunningham did not seek nor was he given that path, but he wastes no time in regrets. Though his sorrow over his solitude is a palpable presence throughout the documentary, much greater is his unbounded joy at taking up his camera and hitting the streets, in search of beauty, alone. In his speech accepting the award of Chevalier of the French Academy of Arts and Sciences, speaking a hilarious mélange of English and really bad French, he says through tears, "He who seeks beauty will find it." The moment makes me squirm, but in a true and necessary way. He is one of those souls about whom Welty wrote that "when somebody, no matter who, gives everything, it makes people feel ashamed."

That kind of radical transparency—the photographer not as capturer of a moment (who can capture a moment?) but as a teacher opening our eyes to a way of looking at and being in the world—could originate only in someone who from earliest consciousness rehearsed being (to use his word) "invisible." And who is best at being invisible? The gay child, the abused child, the wounded child, the misfit, the outlier, the solitary.

I am given to think of any number of seekers of beauty who have been persecuted by those who can't bear the witness they offer to the presence of the sacred in our midst. The Dalai Lama has noted that, had the Buddha lived in a less stable, more violent time and place, he would likely have met the same fate as Jesus, condemned to die for the witness he bore to the world of peace and beauty available to everyone who makes the hard choice to seek it. The most pernicious tool of power is the control of access to beauty—confine it to museums and gated parks and, yes, churches, and charge admission. With every photograph, Cunningham showed us how to find beauty, for free, in our lives, on the street.

CHAPTER 12

From Loneliness to Solitude

NOT LONG AGO I was for several months writer-in-residence at a study-abroad program in Aix, the ancient Roman capital of Provence, where my office window looked onto the façade of Saint-Sauveur, the Aix cathedral. This was the church where, in the final years of his life, Paul Cézanne attended mass every Sunday before walking deeper into the city for dinner with his wife and son. They were among his few human contacts in the week. He lived alone and he painted. He drew his religion, he wrote, from his painting, where he sought to paint the soul in all things, animate and inanimate.

In Aix my apartment was on the fourth floor (no elevator), just a bit lower than the cathedral bell tower, and I was so close to the tower that when the bells rang, I could watch them swing. They formed a chorus and they were serious bells, the cheerful, sweet voices of the tenor bells underlain by the calm, solid foundation of the deep, noble bass bells, all pure in tone, crafted in the sixteenth century, when people paid attention to such things. Waking to them and then basking in their resonance was a transcendent experience. Their vibrations penetrated the bones. I especially liked their afterglow, when the pulling stopped—the variations from one day to the next convinced me the bell ropes were pulled manually—but the bells kept ringing, and ringing, and ringing, and ringing, and . . . then there was one solitary little ring, always a tenor bell, like a sigh, and then silence, though the bells were still vibrating and for another minute their wonderful and particular harmonic hum filled my room.

Three times daily, at appointed hours—the times fixed for prayer—the bells rang solemnly, with one tenor and one bass bell put into service. But on Saturdays, couples traveled from throughout the south of France to marry here for the pleasure and drama of emerging from the grand ogival doors, framed by a parade of statues of saints and overseen by the winged Saint Michael, patron of France, piercing his demon at the apex of the façade. Even sequestered deep in the apartment, away from the windows, I recognized weddings by the reckless pealing, as the full complement of bells rang.

I doubt they pealed for Cézanne, who married Hortense after many years, well after their son was born. For certain they will never peal for solitaries like me. I considered this more than once as I sat bathed in their music, working at my desk. My life as a solitary—as necessary, I insist, as any other life—will never be so joyously, dramatically, and communally celebrated.

And so I have written this book, to study, learn from, and celebrate the lives of those who have been chosen by or who choose solitude, and to investigate the roots of my affection for being alone.

The act of creation is a reaching out. Consider possibly the most famous act of creation in art, painted by Michelangelo, that solitary among solitaries, in which a great, gray-bearded God extends his life-giving touch to Adam on the ceiling of the Sistine Chapel: one solitude reaching out to another. That Adam took the gift of life for granted is only human nature, but my solitaries—sparrows who of little love knew how to starve—did not take the gift of life for granted. This is the lesson they teach through their lives and their art—if only I will listen.

On the day my father lay in his funeral home coffin for visitation, Ott and Duck Burks, bachelor solitaries who lived in the hills, were the first to arrive. They wore their best clothes—matching bib overalls, faded to pale blue but recently washed. Ott had a snow-white beard flowing to his chest, with two ineradicable tobacco stains at the corners of his mouth. They climbed the funeral home steps humbly and in awe. They were acutely aware that in town they were out of their element, out of the woods, and they were from the Protestant side of the river, where church was a whitewashed wood frame box with a single bare cross. The glamor and gore of Roman Catholicism was something that, even in their advanced years, even though they lived five miles from a Catholic town and county, they had encountered mostly in rumor and hearsay. "Mr. Johnson was a fine man," one said, "and we come to pay our respects."

To encounter such unselfconscious, plainspoken, heartfelt emotion was a lifetime education in a moment, as was their discomfort and befuddlement at the funeral home's array of icons and idols. My father abhorred funerals—he would have had us bury him in the garden or, better yet, in the woods he roamed and loved. The funeral was for my mother, to keep up appearances and provide a mourning ritual, but in deference to my father's sensibilities, if not his wishes, his children had the coffin closed. For Ott and Duck, a closed coffin meant only one thing. "Were he in a *car wreck*?" Duck blurted out. Then there was the kneeler by the coffin, whose function was obvious but too popish for their Southern, Protestant souls; and then the ritual of the guest book, and I am certain that neither had held a pen in many years.

Townspeople on their way to work, wearing clothes bought at the mall instead of at Howard's Gen'l. Mdse., began stopping by. Ott and Duck were soon gone, and their world and that of my father gone not much later. Too many people populate the hills now for them to roam free—too many roads, too many rules. But the memory of these two bachelor, solitary brothers remains, along with the purity of the affection they held for my father and a strain of backwoods wildness I recognize, however attenuated, in myself. That purity of heart is something to aspire to. That innocence—not at all the same as naiveté—is a worthwhile goal.

What the subjects of these pages have in common: each lost the self to find the self. Thoreau lost himself in the woods surrounding Walden Pond. Cézanne lost himself to his painting and to his beloved Mont Sainte-Victoire. Welty lost herself in her art—writing and photography; Tagore in his music, his poetry, his students, in the many mouths of the Ganges; Simone in her music. Capitalism tells me I will find myself in things—I will locate my self, literally and psychologically, in and with my phone—when what my solitaries have taught me, again and again in their different ways, is that if I want to find the self, give it away, again and again, until there is no more left.

I have come to delight, not only in my solitude but in my loneliness, its shape and texture, its undulations, how it changes from day to day, a relationship in its own right—a relationship with the self, with the imagination, with my work. There I feel a visceral connection to some deep, enduring truth that I can access only in the silence of my heart, in the silence of this room, where I write first drafts in pen and ink on the verso side of already-used paper—this last consideration is so essential that, when traveling, I pack a few already-used pages. Writing on already-used paper provides the liberation of playtime— the composted and tilled garden of all revelation. I am daily and endlessly grateful for books, portable wisdom; every room of my small house is papered with the color and variety of their spines, each book evidence of its writer's hours of contemplation, labor, solitude. I write among them as a student among teachers.

This is the magic of the word in print: not that it answers questions but that it composes an ongoing score for life, a mute chorus of voices as alive and evolving as light.

Silence and solitude set the imagination free to roam, which may be why capitalism devotes itself so assiduously to creating crowds and noise. Wisdom begins in listening; listening begins in silence; silence is rooted in solitude. Asked to speak of her love for her father in Shakespeare's *King Lear*, Cordelia, youngest of Lear's daughters, whose love is so great she will not taint it with flattery, remains silent. But silence is not nothing. The solitary's love, so often expressed in restraint, so often acted out in silence, is no less important than the publicly declared and celebrated love of spouses, parents, children, or siblings.

The connection between solitude and silence is not inevitable—returning from a busy day, solitaries may turn on the television as or more often than their coupled counterparts—but solitude achieves fulfillment in silence. I possess an interior voice that experience has taught me to heed and yet that still too often I ignore. To hear that voice, I sit down, shut up, and listen.

To return to the question that started our journey: what is the usefulness of the solitary?

One use of the solitary, it turns out, is to be useless. What would be lost if every Welty short story and Dickinson poem, every Cézanne painting or Nina Simone recording were lost? The question is not idle. After his brother-in-law sold many of the paintings Cézanne had stored in his father's house, Cézanne burned those that were left. Dickinson's sister Lavinia burned her correspondence, as Emily had instructed, but instead of destroying her poems, Lavinia set about finding a publisher. As for Nina Simone, audio recording is recent technology; had she sung a century earlier, to know her voice would have required being present for her singing.

Why sing? Why paint or dance? Why write? What could be more useless? Why make time to be alone, when the device on which I'm

typing sells itself as a means to banish solitude? In uselessness—
in being in place in solitude—I am most present to what Chekhov
called the "unceasing movement toward perfection"—my fundamen-
tal belonging to all that is.

Both Cézanne and Émile Zola, friends in their youth, evolved toward
solitude—Cézanne painting alone in his studio or on the slopes of
Mont Sainte-Victoire, and Zola, though a public figure at the center
of the political and social life of France, identifying himself as a solitary. Recalling their youth, Zola wrote to his friend, "For ten years
we have talked art and literature. We often lived together—do you
remember?—and often daybreak surprised us, discussing still, rifling
the past, questioning the present, endeavoring to discover the truth
and to create for ourselves an infallible, total religion. We shifted
horrendous piles of ideas, we examined and rejected all systems, and,
after such hard labor, we said to ourselves that beyond the powerful
and individual life there is nothing but lies and stupidity." Together,
from opposite ends of the political spectrum, they arrived at the
same conclusion, this blunt truth I shelter in my heart: "beyond the
powerful and individual life there is nothing but lies and stupidity."

"Is being alone really living?" van Gogh asks in a letter to his
brother and best friend, Theo. A paragraph later he answers his question: "This much I believe about you, and this much I know about
myself . . . there is a foundation of serenity . . . so that neither of us
is unhappy, our serenity being based on the fact that we truly and
sincerely love our trade and our work, and that art occupies a large
part of our hearts and makes life interesting." Van Gogh gave an even

more eloquent response, of course, in his paintings. "I want to do drawings that will *touch* some people," he writes. In that he surely succeeded, and if he never knew or suspected the magnitude of his success, of what consequence, finally, is that, when one understands being an artist as not about making product for a market but as a way of life.

In *Solitude: A Return to the Self*, British psychiatrist Anthony Storr cites Freud's comment that psychological health relies on the ability to love *and* to work. "We have over-emphasized the former," Storr writes, "and paid too little attention to the latter." That exclusive emphasis on romantic love is a response to the impoverishment of work, as capitalism and technology rob us of the satisfactions to be found in a task well done, whether growing my own food or entertaining myself with my own thoughts and voice. I surround myself with devices that clean my floors, plot my course, give me information, supply me with prefabricated stories—commandeering my powers of imagination, leaving me without anything to do for myself. And so, lacking inner resources, I am lonely.

Storr points out that we owe to Freud and his fellow Victorians the concept that heterosexual sex within the context of marriage is the gold standard of human contentment. As Storr observes, "Some of the people who have contributed most to the enrichment of human experience have contributed little to the welfare of human beings in particular." Indeed, solitaries have traditionally been of greater service to society—to our communities—than to their immediate relatives or social circles. Rather than focus itself on a single individual or blood kin, the solitary's love diffuses itself in many channels, like a great river as it approaches the sea.

My solitaries illuminate the difference between narcissism and solitude: a brushstroke by Cézanne or van Gogh, a sentence by Eudora Welty, a phrase sung by Nina Simone, a silence shaped by Erik Satie, a photograph by Bill Cunningham. The narcissist wants to be admired through the work; the solitary is content in its making.

A friend who knows I'm writing in praise of solitude asks me, kindly but pointedly, "What's wrong with two people deciding to take care of each other for life?" People can promise to care for each other for life, I responded, without state- and church-certified marriage, though our society offers no support for such arrangements. But, I continued, I had experienced a community in crisis where *we all took care of one another*—the gay, lesbian, and transgender communities of San Francisco in the 1980s and early 1990s, the first years of the AIDS epidemic—in no small part because *no one was married.* American University law professor Nancy Polikoff described an analogous situation among the women's community of the time: "A friend died of breast cancer, and her blood family arrived for the funeral. They were astounded to discover that their daughter had a group of people who were a family, who'd been providing support—somebody had organized a schedule, somebody brought food every night. In some ways it was the absence of marriage as a dominant institution that created space for the development of a family defined in much broader ways." I do not think the collective, community caregiving models that evolved in the early years of the AIDS epidemic would happen today, in large part because now gay men and lesbians can marry. Opening to one has replaced opening to all.

Virginia Woolf perceived this evolution and wickedly satirized it in her novel *Orlando*. During several centuries abroad, Orlando transforms from a man to a woman in an apotheosis that takes place in a Turkish harem. Then she returns home to Victorian England, to be unsettled by the change that has taken place in her absence:

> It now seemed to her that the whole world was ringed with gold. . . . Wedding rings abounded. She went to church. Wedding rings were everywhere. . . . Couples trudged and plodded in the middle of the road indissolubly linked together. The woman's right hand was invariably passed through the man's left and her fingers were gripped by his. . . . Orlando could only suppose that some new discovery had been made about the race; they were somehow stuck together, couple after couple, but who had made it, and when, she could not guess. . . . It was strange—it was distasteful; indeed, there was something in this dissolubility of bodies which was repugnant to her sense of decency and sanitation.

In an interview, the pioneering French scholar of human sexuality and behavior Michel Foucault described the institutionalization of affection while calling for alternatives:

> We live in a relational world that institutions have considerably impoverished. Society and the institutions which frame it have limited the possibility of relationships because a rich relational world would be very complex to manage. We should fight against the impoverishment of the relational fabric. . . . The single person must be recognized as having relations with others quite different from those of a married couple . . .

Foucault is an idealist, but without an ideal to strive toward as a goal and measuring stick, we are lost. The best marriages of my acquaintance are indifferent to church and state; they are allegiances between solitaries, where marriage is not a wall but an opening door; they are partnerships of friends. In explaining their decision not to marry, a gay man told me of his partner, "He has promised me nothing and given me everything." That, it strikes me, is a true marriage, a marriage consecrated in the heart.

My childhood home has been sold—the house my father built of old bricks I helped scrape, the house with my now barely-discernible handprint in the cement lip surrounding the fire pit, the house with the bourbon-mash-soaked, tongue-and-groove cypress paneling and my mother's greenhouse and the three-ton rock altar that will mystify archeologists ten thousand years hence. The paperwork was signed at a meeting to which all the siblings were invited except me, the only unmarried child. When I found out, I thought of Cézanne's brother-in-law selling Jas de Bouffan, Cézanne's childhood home and his painting studio for much of his life, along with the paintings Cézanne had stored there. They brought a few francs each. Cézanne took his share of the money from the sale of the house and built his *atélier* north of Aix. Cézanne is buried in his family plot in Aix, within view of Mont Sainte-Victoire; his wife is buried in the Cimitière Père Lachaise in Paris, the city of her birth, which suited her tastes far better than provincial Aix.

The situations, mine and Cézanne's, are as different as an intervening century and ocean might suggest. I had many opportunities to buy my parents' house; I declined for reasons that still make sense, even gilded by the patina of memory. All the same, the loss of the anchor, the bedrock, the labor of my blood family's collective hands is a dagger to the heart that wakes me in the middle of the night in far-flung places. Whatever objections one may have to fortress marriage, by definition it provides a fortress. For all my life, the house in the Kentucky hills had served that role. With it gone, I run the solitary's risk of becoming so detached from any mooring that I am lost to the ever-changing currents of life.

> It is a business of the very few to be independent; it is a privilege of the strong. . . . He enters into a labyrinth, he multiplies a thousandfold the dangers which life in itself already brings with it; not least of which is that no one can see how and where he loses his way, becomes isolated, and is torn piecemeal by some minotaur of conscience. . . . And he cannot any longer go back!
>
> Friedrich Nietzsche, *Beyond Good and Evil*

At twenty-four, Nietzsche became the youngest person to hold a chair at the University of Basel. At thirty-four, he had to retire; a hereditary neurological disorder was ravaging his health. Ten years later he collapsed, losing his mind but living another eleven years under the care first of his mother, then his sister, who took the opportunity to rework his manuscripts into a perspective more in keeping with her own anti-Semitism and sympathy for fascism. Not until after her death were his intentions restored.

Nietzsche's story is not cheerful, but one does not become a philosopher, or an artist, or a writer, in search of a cheerful story;

one goes in search of one's truth, using the means fate has offered, and accepts responsibility for the consequences. In his 1950s' best-seller *The Outsider*, Colin Wilson described the outsider as someone "who cannot live in the comfortable, insulated world of the bourgeois . . . It is not simply the need to cock a snook at respectability that provokes [the outsider]; it is a distressing sense that truth must be told at all costs." Nietzsche is one of Wilson's outsiders; he was also, not coincidentally, a solitary. No one is more avoided in life—if admired after death—than she or he who must tell the truth "at all costs."

In a society obsessed with coupling (turn on the radio and try to find a song that's not about true love—getting it, wanting it, losing it, getting it back), the solitary acts as a contemporary court jester, telling truths about our communities that those certified by the laws of state and church are unable to perceive or unwilling to speak aloud. In this Cassandra, the seer of Greek mythology, is the very patroness of solitude and solitaries. When she refuses Apollo's advances, he spits in her mouth. (Ain't that just like a man.) Afterward she always speaks the truth, but no one listens.

I seek communities grounded not in government-sanctioned marriage but in friendship, because, as partners to every successful marriage know, friendship can survive without marriage but healthy marriage cannot long endure without friendship.

Why don't the entertainment industry and religious institutions support more songs, books, movies praising friendship? Because friendship, unlike marriage, offers no capital to church, state, and corporation. There is no profit to be made or power to be gained from a relationship founded not in property but in respect and affection.

Could we not elevate friendship so that in our imaginations it is on a par with marriage? Could we broaden and enrich our feast of love—our "relational institutions"—so that the tower bells of the cathedral of Saint-Sauveur ring not just for weddings, but to celebrate love in all its manifestations? I'm thinking of a spinster I know in a small town in eastern Kentucky, who works as a nurse in a clinic serving people without health insurance and who led a battle against surface mining—successful for the moment—in the watershed where her family has lived for two centuries. In my imagination, her community would come together in a ritual devised to celebrate her lifelong, selfless giving.

These days many of us have come to understand meditation, contemplation, prayer—different labels for similar practices—not as vehicles for masochism and self-punishment but as means of transformation, tools for spiritual and psychological growth. And yet perhaps the transformation we seek is toward a greater appreciation of the virtues of asceticism—or, to use Marianne Moore's word, restraint—transforming our attitude toward solitude from unease to tenderness and respect. We reject asceticism as a punitive tool in favor of practicing it as the key to the discipline of living within our means—of true freedom, where we are servants not to anonymous corporate entities but to one another.

Instead of comfort and distraction, I use solitude as the seeker uses a fast—to hone and sharpen, to engage the self and in doing so to break through the illusion of aloneness and emerge with my compassion and engagement with the world deepened and enriched. Through solitude, in contradiction to every message from our security-obsessed, wall-building society, I seek to open my heart.

In *On Disobedience,* the solitary philosopher Erich Fromm, who described himself as a "nontheistic mystic," writes, "In order to disobey, one must have the courage to be alone, to err, and to sin. But courage is not enough. . . . Only if a person . . . has emerged as a fully developed individual and has thus acquired the capacity to think and feel for himself, only then can he have the capacity to say 'no' to power, to disobey." And later, "The capacity to doubt, to criticize, and to disobey may be all that stands between a future for mankind and the end of civilization." In our era of global warming and its attendant social and cultural disruptions, Fromm's message has become even more imperative.

That is why it is so important to teach and appreciate the joy to be found in solitude. In silence and in solitude I cultivate "the courage to be alone." In silence and in solitude I stand my best chance of emerging as a "fully developed individual [who can] think and feel" for myself.

A retired biology teacher, school principal, and widow whom I met in the south of France told me, when I asked after her three daughters, that they all live in the north. "But I chose to live down here," she said. "I like the sun, and I like to swim, and I like being near the sea. I could live up north, nearer to them, but I visit them when I wish and I am happy here because *this is what I chose.*" She says these last words with the emphasis of a working mother who for most of her life was responsible for others' lives, and is now fulfilled in being responsible to her own. It is the opportunity to *shape* her destiny that she enjoys. Now she is a mother-in-place for students abroad, teaching them language, culture, and customs. She has continued her service in solitude.

In my twenties, I decided I would not father children, a decision that, along with falling in love in my thirties with a terminally ill man, has taught me most about sorrow and loss. I see my siblings' or friends' features in their children, or, in their adopted children, the repetition of a gesture or speech pattern learned from their parent. I feel the depth, even in its challenges, of their relationships and, yes, of their marriages.

But then the forest and the open sky remind me that I belong to all creatures as they belong to me, that to understand only biological offspring as our children is to shortchange the great human impulse toward magnanimity, toward altruism. In the classroom, in my creative writing workshops—in which many of my students devote themselves to healing damage done to them by their biological parents—I experience with my students a different kind of love, the love of learning, the love of a good story, well told.

Solitude and silence are the hero's journey, voluntarily undertaken to achieve a greater goal. From George Bernard Shaw's play *Saint Joan,* his adaptation of the transcripts from the heresy trial of Joan of Arc:

> JOAN: Do not think you can frighten me by telling me that I am alone. France is alone; and God is alone; and what is my loneliness before the loneliness of my country and my God?

I see now that the loneliness of God is His strength . . . Well, my loneliness shall be my strength too; it is better to be alone with God; His friendship will not fail me, nor His counsel, nor His love. In His strength I will dare, and dare, and dare, until I die.

The Buddha and Jesus sacrificed their comfortable and secure lives to cultivate solitude, leaving their homes and taking to the road; both undertook extended periods of solitude before presuming to teach. But the hero's journey need not be literal, to lead armies or decamp to the foothills of the Himalayas or bear the cross to Golgotha. The path may be followed at home, at the desk or the canvas, in the armchair or the garden. "I am a writer who came of a sheltered life," wrote Eudora Welty. "A sheltered life can be a daring life as well. For all serious daring starts from within." The solitary self is the vehicle, the ship that takes us on the interior journey from loneliness to solitude.

In a 1970s' interview with James Baldwin on British television, the interviewer remarks, "When you were starting out as a writer, you were black, impoverished, homosexual. You must have said to yourself, 'Gee—how disadvantaged can I get?'" To which Baldwin responds, "Oh, no, I thought I hit the jackpot! It was so outrageous you could not go any further. So you had to find a way to use it."

To be born bent, however that manifested itself, was once to be forced to look within—to explore and express what seems different in yourself. The child born to bent sexuality, women born in almost any society, had no choice in this interior searching. Since the exterior world was so hostile, we turned inside. As a result, journals and memoirs became one of our primary means of growth and expression—even as until recently the gatekeepers of the academy dismissed them as unworthy of being called literature or taught in the classroom.

Our outlier status—our solitude—was a wellspring of creativity. The solitaries I have profiled understood commitment as well as or better than any marriage vow undertaken with the knowledge of no-fault divorce waiting in the wings. Their lifelong, selfless practice rooted itself in their fecund, uneasy difference: their queerness and their solitude. These writers and artists took unbreakable vows to their art, dedicating their lives to showing us, their audiences, the human condition. Through their art they showed us that the solitude we so fear is an illusion, a scrim preventing us from seeing how we are all in this boat together, we are all one.

In spring 2017, for the first time since publishing a memoir set at the height of San Francisco's AIDS epidemic, I taught a course in memoir—which is to say, at least as I taught it, a course in the necessity of personal witness, the interior journey; a course against forgetting. On the last day, I asked my students, several of whom were married, which they thought more important: marriage or friendship. Thirteen of fourteen favored friendship, a response I found so incredible that I asked them to keep their hands up while I counted a second time. In their raised hands I find hope; I hear the voice of Walt Whitman's cameradoes:

As I lay with my head in your lap, camerado,

The confession I made I resume—what I said to you in the
open air I resume:

I know I am restless, and make others so;

. . . For I confront peace, security, and all the settled laws,
to unsettle them . . .

. . . Dear camerado! I confess I have urged you onward with
me, and still urge you, without the least idea what is our
destination,

Or whether we shall be victorious, or utterly quell'd and
defeated.

Throughout his life, Whitman envisioned a community of cameradoes, a brotherhood and sisterhood of humankind. On the other
side of the Atlantic, Vincent van Gogh's first letter from Provence
to his brother Theo presents an elaborate plan for a collective of
artists who would pool their resources, improving prices for their
work while also helping the "whole battalion of artists who have been
working in unremitting poverty." "I think every day about this artists' association," he writes. Degas, Monet, Renoir, and Pissarro were
among those he hoped would join forces in a collective shout, saying,
"Our pictures belong *to the artists!*"

Van Gogh, who from early on tried to live by Jesus's words, whose
efforts to give himself to others went wrong again and again, offers
a textbook case against such idealism—until I look at his paintings,
which bear silent witness to the power and importance and necessity
of his love, not for one person but for everything and all.

Like Whitman, like van Gogh, I have searched all my life for
a community of friends, living in proximity, sharing resources and

caregiving. Like Whitman, like van Gogh, I will not find it, but I have felt more deeply because of the search; it has served as Polaris for my heart, and the search has made my journey worthwhile.

On one of my visits to the Abbey of Gethsemani, I spoke with Brother Martin DeLoach, an African American Trappist monk to whom my father taught plumbing and whom he sponsored for certification in the local plumbers' union, thereby enabling Martin to make a place for himself in the monastic life he so loved. "That's what makes a monk, you know," Martin told me. "Alone with God, and finally we're all monks, every one of us, because we can be as social as we want but when it gets to that last moment we're all going to be alone." When crises come, though friends and relatives may be generous and eager to help, in the end it is I, alone on the trail, alone in the museum, alone in the courtroom, alone in the emergency room, alone in the morgue, alone in my illness, alone in my reading, alone in my writing, alone in the silence of my heart. I, I, I, the Doric column of the English alphabet—the software insists on upper case—the centrality, in our language, at least, of the first person.

The spinster Marianne Moore quoted the theologian Martin Buber: "The free man believes in destiny and knows that it has need of him." "Not *fate*," Moore adds, "destiny." Fate is what has chosen me; destiny is what I make of it. *Fate* suggests submission to the circumstances of life; *destiny* suggests active engagement. The former implies some all-powerful force or figure to whose will I must submit, and before whose power I am helpless. The latter implies that I am a manifestation of one of the infinite aspects of creation, whose fullest expression depends in some small but necessary way on my day-to-day, moment-to-moment decisions. The fully realized solitary takes fate and sculpts it into a destiny.

Some are called to marry; some are called to solitude; some are called to one or the other way of being at different points of our lives. I use the passive construction deliberately. Whether one chooses to assign a name to the summoning force is a matter of personal preference; I favor ancient formulations that placed a taboo on the use of a name or word. But an order prevails, however humans mock, violate, or ignore it. Consciously or otherwise, I seek to balance what has chosen me—fate—with what I have chosen—destiny. That the former is of greater consequence I do not doubt, but I also do not doubt that we each have a role to play in turning the wheel. For me, for now, solitude is the best means by which to discern and act out that role.

If the great experiment in the primacy of individual identities and rights is to have meaning beyond ravaging the planet to secure ever-greater market share, it must identify and seek not a *fate*, but a *destiny*. We are caught—trapped, some might say—in the web of fate, but just as surely we are each among its multitude of spinners. In our spinning lies our hope; in our spinning lies our destinies. Just as marriages or partnerships are not given but made, solitaries can consciously embrace and inhabit our solitude. Cézanne trusted no learning he did not come by himself. Welty writes that she was always her own teacher. In her story "Music from Spain," she describes a Spanish guitar player performing in San Francisco:

. . . the life of an artist, or a foreigner, or a wanderer [were finally] all the same thing . . . Were the difficulties and challenges what he [the guitar player] sought for most? . . . not bothering to conceal his absorption in what he was playing, the man took no notice or care that he pleased anyone else either . . . passion was the thing he had in hand; love was his servant, and even despair was a tamed little animal trotting about in plain view.

Welty's choice of disciplines is telling—a guitar player, like a short story writer or essayist, has little hope of large-scale fame or hefty remuneration. The guitarist (the artist, the foreigner, the wanderer, the solitary) plays in service to beauty, for the challenge of pouring his life and soul into forms as infinite and rich as life itself—seeking, in fact, an entryway to suffering, seeking "the difficulties and challenges." In solitude, one may learn how to play one's consciousness like an instrument, in the way that singers train their voices or painters train their eyes. The guitarist turns all suffering, even love, even darkness and despair, to the end of creating beauty. Through his commitment to his art, he makes a better world for you and me, but that is not his first concern. He is first in service to the discipline of beauty.

Intelligent design or, if you prefer, concatenation of circumstance and frequent flier miles brought me repeatedly to my aged mother, under the care of the good Sisters of Loretto, as I was researching and writing these pages. On a good day—these were fewer and farther apart—she told stories of driving Thomas Merton (Father Louis to her) to the train station in the family's battered red Ford Country Squire. Those stories provoked another story, of the return of Merton's body after his death by accidental electrocution in his Bangkok hotel room. The body remained in Thailand almost a week before being loaded into a military transport plane, Merton the pacifist, mystic monk in his shiny black body bag amid a hundred and more dead soldiers in their shiny black body bags—an image of solitude amid unity if ever one was known. Merton's body arrived at Fort Knox and was delivered to the funeral home in my small town for identification. The coroner called in my father, together with several monks, but after more than a week in a tropical country the body was too decomposed to identify except by its false teeth, which are still, or so my mother believes, in Merton's dentist's possession.

Then she segued to her story of Merton's funeral, where, as the body was lowered into the earth—the advanced decomposition necessitated a coffin, a departure from the usual Trappist practice of burial in nothing more than formal robes—a woman in a long black veil ran from the knoll of plain white crosses, across a meadow dusted white with December snow and hail. "Joan Baez," my mother said confidently, and I chose to believe her. It was 1968, a year in which such things happened.

Now, visiting those crosses as the Abbey's great bell tolls the hours to wake the dead, I realize that the monastery cemetery holds the greatest concentration of the dead of my life, greater even than the Golden Gate, repository for the ashes of so many friends dead of AIDS. Here at Gethsemani I find crosses for Alfred, Alban, Guerric, Giles, Stephen, Claude, Wilfrid, Patrick, Martin, Thomas, Matthew, Louis—Father Louis—and buried not here but in my heart, those monks who returned to the secular world: Lavrans, Donald, Clement, who gave his birth name John as my first name, and Fintan, who devised the fruitcake recipe that made the abbey prosperous and to whom, in his offering me a role model, I may owe my calling to solitude.

I imagine and propose solitaries as models for the choice of reverence over irony. Instead of conquering nations or mountains or outer space, we set out to conquer our need to conquer. If that seems a tall order, I offer Walt Whitman, our national saint, who taught us how to be American. Emily Dickinson, his sister in solitude and sainthood, who taught us how to be alive to the world, most especially to the suffering of its solitaries. I offer Paul Cézanne, painting in solitude six days of seven, painting himself to the point of diabetic collapse, reinventing painting. Henry James, portraying the caustic corruptions of fortress marriage, living alone in Lamb House by the sea. Zora Neale Hurston, who nurtured a flame of mysticism in a world hostile to it, and who showed that through her wits alone a woman, a black woman, could break her chains, and who died in poverty and was buried in an unmarked grave in a potter's field. Rabindranath Tagore, preserving and furthering the ideal of an education dedicated not to profit but to beauty. I offer Eudora Welty, writing magical realism when Gabriel García Márquez was a teenager. I offer you Bill Cunningham, who took photographs from exuberance—from his insatiable love of the created world. I offer you Jesus, that renegade proto-feminist communitarian bachelor Jew, who reminded us of the lesson set forth a thousand years earlier in the Hebrews' holy book:

to love our neighbors as ourselves. I offer you Siddhartha Gautama, who sat in solitude for seven years to achieve the understanding that everyone and everything are one.

The multiplication of our society's demons has been accompanied by a ratcheting up of the sources and volume of its background noise. The chatter and diversions of our lives (Twitter, Facebook, Instagram, texts . . .) serve to keep the demons at bay, even as we are creating demons faster than we can create noise to drown them out: environmental devastation, global warming, the growing gap between the rich and the poor, uncontrolled population growth, unlimited consumption held up by international media and most of our leaders as the glittering purpose of life.

The appropriate response is not more noise. The appropriate response is more silence.

To choose to be alone is to bait the trap, to create a space the demons cannot resist entering. And that's the good news; the demons that enter can be named, written about, and tamed through the miracle of the healing word, the miracle of art, the miracle of silence.

"I find ecstasy in living; the mere sense of living is joy enough," wrote Dickinson. That joy, that ecstasy that Dickinson describes—I know that it is not limited to celibates or solitaries, but I also know that it shows itself to us in particular ways denied those who are coupled. Visions appear to the solitary prophet. Revelations arrive in silence and solitude. The deepest feeling shows itself in restraint.

Only in solitude could my solitaries become teachers for you and me, teachers for and of the universe. Like Jesus, bachelor for the ages, they keep ever before me the ideal toward which I may strive. They raise the bar of what it means to be alive. By striving toward their ideal I stand a chance of becoming better than I thought myself capable of being.

Hanging by my door, I keep a mask in the style of the Eskimo (a term many Arctic Natives use) or Inuit (more appropriate for outsiders), the face somewhere between recognizably human and fantastically animal, though to write as much is to acknowledge what the Inuit knew and Anglos have misplaced or forgotten, which is that *we* are animals—citizens, however badly socialized, of the animal kingdom. The mask was made by Brother Claude Jungwirth, whose last name I provide because, like so many of the Trappist monks' surnames, it recalls the great immigrant communities of the upper Midwest, who clung to their religion and their faith as a way of grounding themselves in a new and foreign land.

I know little about Brother Claude. The care and precision of the execution of the mask makes clear that he was a skilled woodworker, ten years my father's senior and so possibly his carpentering mentor. Claude was not among the monks who came regularly to my parents' house, but the house held a number of gifts from his woodworking hands; he and my father must have been close. That wordless relationship, grounded in the labor of his hands, was how my father loved and, to the extent he permitted, accepted love in return. Only now, after the house he built has left my family, do I fully understand how thoroughly he incarnated his love in his work. Every brick, board, and nail in its construction passed through his hands or under his eyes.

Claude's mask intrigues me in its abstraction. I have as well from his hand a stylized bird that is a swoop of walnut carved to follow the grain—not a particular bird but rather an essence of bird. Evidently he was drawn to the basic form as much or more than to detail. He did not carve the mask by my door as a decorative object but, for a devout man, as a totem. What precisely was its significance to him lies buried with Claude and perhaps with my father; since the mask was Claude's gift, they may have discussed its significance, though I have difficulty imagining my father speaking about the intimate emotions we wear masks to conceal.

In my childhood I did not know there was such a thing as homophobia; I did not know that gay people existed. I knew that some essential aspect of my character was deeply, irretrievably bent, and that my very survival required that I hide it, whatever it was, at all costs, but I did not know enough to know what it was I was required to hide. I recall clearly the first time I heard the word "cocksucker"—seventh grade, summer evening, bank steps, caution light, where I'd joined the local boys hanging out in a hopeless effort to figure out how to belong, how to be one of them, how not to be a solitary. My cousin said the word not as a particular insult to a particular person but in a generic way that embraced all foul and degrading human behavior. Until that moment I had thought that, with enough control, I could be other than who I was; the mind could defeat the body. But when my cousin spoke the word aloud, the thought leapt to mind: *Uh-oh. That's me he's talking about.* I walked home understanding that no effort would bridge the gap between me and others. I was, in Zora Neale Hurston's apt metaphor, a soundless island in a tideless sea. I would have to make and wear a mask.

And yet neither Claude nor my father nor I would confine

the mask's significance to sexual identity. Both men were at once more innocent and more sophisticated than that. The Inuit saw such masks as enabling the wearer to communicate with the spirit world. "Give a man a mask and he will tell the truth," wrote Oscar Wilde. In their different ways, Claude and my father would have understood the mask to say something about the profound, vast, and finally mysterious nature of reality—the spirit world, the world of solitaries and solitude—behind and beyond the world of appearances, the illusions of empiricism that contemporary developed societies will go to almost any length to maintain. In this the lesson of the mask—its invocation of a world behind and beyond the surface, a world in which I had lived since earliest consciousness—was a tremendous gift.

The efforts we make to glimpse the reality behind the mask—understanding, of course, that the mask itself is one aspect of that reality—we call religion, that which, in the ideal, at least, binds us together with the gods. And—with full and necessary and sorrowful acknowledgment of institutionalized religion's evils, horrors, and omissions—perhaps the exploded and fragmented nature of the contemporary developed world owes itself to the insistence of institutionalized religion and science alike that we subscribe to doctrine and dogma in service to their aggrandizement, instead of attending to the need to bring us together to acknowledge all that is sacred, in ourselves and in our world.

If one accepts that the physics that govern the universe also govern our world—if one "believes in physics," as Einstein wrote, if one believes that the elemental forces of physics that brought the stars into being also act on and through us—then an analogy is implied, however fanciful, between the starry night and the human condition.

In this thought experiment, solitaries correspond to our sun—which is, in astronomical terms, an outlier, as the majority of stars travel in pairs or multiples—while couples correspond to binary star systems: two stars circling each other, bound by their mutual gravitational pull into a single unit. Perhaps the celestial ratio of solitaries to binaries to polyamorous stars might correspond to the ratio of solitary and coupled and polyamorous individuals on our more mortal earth.

If we understood that the earth is of us, as we are of it, maybe we would treat it better. If we understood that there is no shelter from the world and that we are each and every one born to solitude and that this is the good news, maybe we would take more care to create and sustain a cleaner, quieter, slower, gentler world. Conscious of our solitudes, maybe we would be kinder to one another and to our earth. Perhaps that is what the French philosopher Blaise Pascal meant when he wrote that "all humanity's problems stem from an inability to sit in a quiet room alone."

When I imagine my death, I do not see myself surrounded by loved ones with music gently playing in the background, in a hospital or a hospice or even in my rooms, wherever they may be. I see myself alone. Animals, who are so much wiser than we and who so often know their time to die, do not seek out their owners or playmates or offspring, but find a remote corner or glade where they can accomplish this most private act in solitude.

In death I see myself alone, in a landscape where there is still winter. In my imagination I am standing outside the house in Kentucky, the house my parents built. On a cold clear night after a great tongue of arctic air from Canada has passed through and the stars glitter against the infinitude of night, I set out to walk the half-mile or so to the river, the humble Rolling Fork of my childhood, crossing the flagstone patio, past the limestone table and the shop and the dead brown stalks of the frostbitten garden, climbing the fence— some advance planning is called for here, since the aged joints will balk—walking over the frozen rutted field toward the bare-branched water maples and sycamores that line the riverbank—trees that have populated my novels. There must be a moon, so let us have a moon, rising full over the rime-frosted fields, their glitter matching that of the stars. Along the way I shed clothes, pausing long enough to fold each item tenderly and neatly, leaving civilization behind, until I arrive at the river unclothed, naked to the stars. I want to think that I will have courage to do this with no more reinforcement than a shot of bourbon—enough to brighten but not dull the senses—in honor of those who came before and made my life possible, and in hopes that I have accomplished a small measure of the same for those who follow. There you will find my body come the cold, bright blue morning, leaning against the great mottled sycamore of my dreams, happy to have left this world as I came into it, alone but not alone, content to join the company of those who have gone before, who made me who I am and who welcomed me back with open arms to our true and perfect home.

I take hope in every politician's or economist's statement that Americans aren't buying enough; in every student's reference to "sustainability" or "mindfulness"—terms that weren't in my college vocabulary; in the expansion of the concept and increasing use of "queer," founded in a shared resistance to the dominant model: the glorification of greed. I take hope from the growing number of solitaries and the growing interest in meditation, contemplation, centering prayer. I have faith in the capacity of truth, *if brought to light and given time,* to win its cause, the capacity of love to win its cause.

I place little hope in conventional politics, so invested are mainstream political parties in endless, unsustainable growth, or in conventional religion, with its interest in perpetuating its power. Instead I find hope in love, for one another, for our earth. Those of us invested in love can choose, *must* choose noncooperation. I buy less; I consume less; I take myself off the grid in the face of efforts to force me to remain on it; I dedicate myself to friendship as my organizing, bedrock relationship; I study and talk about how to become, in fact, a society of friends.

Conventional economics, conventional politics, and conventional religion are not going to rescue us from ourselves. Can we afford to continue to cultivate and inhabit this age of irony, with our minds separated from our incarnate bodies and the world in which we live? In place of our age of consumption and noise and distraction, I imagine an age of solitude and silence, chosen in full embrace of the knowledge of science, even as it grounds itself in the calm conviction that we live and die in mystery, that all human endeavor must begin and end in respect, for ourselves, for one another, for our fellow creatures.

I like to imagine, as proposed by both William James and Thomas Merton, a secular monasticism—a great conversion of manners, in the terminology of the monastic vows—an "opulence in asceticism," to quote Marianne Moore. In this conversion of my imagination, monasteries and motherhouses and retreat centers play a crucial role, as teachers of the contemplative life have learned. One can and must practice solitude at home, but the practice is reinforced and strengthened by periodic retreats into collective solitude. The simple knowledge that such places exist is an inspiration and a solace.

Zoketsu Norman Fischer's online sangha "Everyday Zen" offers one example of integration of solitude and silence into our daily lives. The Christian oblate movement offers another—even as the numbers decline in Christian religious orders, the number of people who have taken vows of allegiance to those orders' principles is growing.

In my brave new world, we celebrate friendship as the queen of virtues, recognized as the foundation for all worthy human connection, including most particularly marriage. We create storylines other than that of the familiar fortress household, wherein each carefully plotted and spaced house reproduces the nation-state in miniature, us (inside) versus them (outside). We open ourselves to love in all its manifestations; we eliminate hierarchies of love. The parent's love of a child, the dog's love of its master, the walker's love of the path, the reader's love of the word in print, the child's love of everything, the son's love of his mother, the daughter's love of her father, the love of friends, and above all the love of self—the heresy of self-love—I seat them all at the great round table of the feast of love, a table that grows larger as more people come to sit, a meal that never exhausts itself, a table where there is room, yes, there is, for those who are married.

If my dream strikes you as utopian, deluded, grandiose, I point to the great failure of politicians to provide a vision sufficiently grand to counter the call to unrestrained consumption trotted out before us at every hour of every day in every popular medium. My vision is no more fantastical than colonies on Mars, solar grids in space, heat transfer from the oceans, impregnable vaults for nuclear waste, carbon dioxide storage under the Great Plains, or any of hundreds of proposals our politicians and research institutions and media take seriously. It requires no trillion-dollar investment in technology, which history teaches us will inevitably generate problems equal to or greater than those it solves.

Merton writes of solitaries that we are "a mute witness, a secret and even invisible expression of love which takes the form of [our] own option for solitude in preference to the acceptance of social fictions." And what love are we solitaries mute witnesses to? The omnipresence of the great Alone, the infinite possibilities of no duality, no separation between you and me, between the speaker and the spoken to, the dancer and his dance, the writer and her reader, people and our earth.

ACKNOWLEDGMENTS
AND THANKS

I GRATEFULLY ACKNOWLEDGE THE support of the Arizona Council for the Arts, whose individual artist grant supported my travel to the homes and studios of solitaries, and to the John Simon Guggenheim Foundation. I express as well my appreciation to my colleagues at the University of Arizona Department of English, for accommodating leaves to research and write. A particular thanks to the Camargo Foundation in Cassis, and to Philip and Laurence Breeden and the Institut Américain Universitaire in Aix-en-Provence, for writing time and space in my beloved France.

I offer thanks to Alane Mason, my editor at Norton, for her encouragement of this sometimes reluctant mule; to Allegra Huston, my most excellent and attentive copyeditor; and to the staff at W. W. Norton, both in New York and in the field. I thank my agent, Ellen Levine, for her enduring support, and her patient and gracious assistant, Martha Wydysh. I acknowledge the contributions of my many manuscript consultants, chief among them Michael Baun, Melanie Beene, Richard Canning, Suzanne Marrs, Greg Miller, Paul Quenon, Lisa Rappoport, and Jean Rukkila. At *Harper's Magazine*, Chris Beha and Ellen Rosenbush offered superb advice. I offer an especially deep bow to Shirley Abbott, deceased as these pages were going to print, in appreciation of her lifelong editorship and our epistolary love; sometimes I think it is the best kind. I hope the final version justifies my readers' intelligence, labor, and love. They brought clarity to my writing and corrected many missteps; I am solely responsible for any that remain.

Portions of this book have been adapted from "Going It Alone: The Dignity and Challenge of Solitude," which appeared in *Harper's Magazine*, April 2015.

"All Serious Daring Begins Within: Eudora Welty" has been adapted from an essay of the same title that appeared in *The Georgia Review*, spring 2012.

PERMISSIONS

"Autobiographia Literaria" from *The Collected Poems of Frank O'Hara* by Frank O'Hara copyright © 1971 by Maureen Granville-Smith, Administratrix of the Estate of Frank O'Hara, copyright renewed 1999 by Maureen O'Hara Granville-Smith and Donald Allen. Used by permission of Alfred A. Knopf, an imprint of the Knopf Double-day Publishing Group, a division of Penguin Random House LLC. All rights reserved.

Excerpts from Eudora Welty correspondence reprinted by the permission of Russell & Volkening as agents for Eudora Welty, copyright © 1941 by Eudora Welty.

Excerpts from *Dust Tracks on a Road* by Zora Neale Hurston © 1942 by Zora Neale Hurston; renewed © 1970 by John C. Hurston. Reprinted by permission of HarperCollins Publishers. UK and Commonwealth (excluding Canada) excerpts reprinted by permission from Little, Brown/UK.